CINDERELLA, YOU BITCH

CINDERELLA, YOU BITCH

RESCUE YOUR RELATIONSHIPS

FROM THE

FAIRY-TALE FANTASY

SHANNON HETH & BEAU NELSON

WONDERWELL

Library of Congress Control Number: 2021915203

ISBN 978-1-63756-002-0 (paperback)
ISBN 978-1-63756-003-7 (EPUB)

Editor: Joanna Henry
Cover design and interior design: Morgan Krehbiel
Cover image: Photo 12 / Alamy Stock Photo
Authors' photo: Amanda Pratt

Published by Wonderwell in Los Angeles, CA
www.wonderwell.press

WONDERWELL

Distributed in the US by Publishers Group West and in Canada by Publishers Group Canada

Printed and bound in Canada

For my mom, the most courageous woman I know.

—SH

To Ella, Lauryn, and Dylan, my little heroines in training:
Uncle Beau loves you.

And to my transformational teachers, Lynne Sheridan and Lisa Kalmin:
I am forever grateful for the light you have shown me.

—BN

CONTENTS

Introduction: Fairy-Tale Fucked | 1

PART ONE ONCE UPON A TIME . . . 11

CHAPTER 1   Once Upon a Time, Fairy Tales Were Pretty Grimm | 13

CHAPTER 2   Mirror, Mirror on the Wall | 29

CHAPTER 3   Princess, That Pattern Does Not Look Good on You | 43

CHAPTER 4   Powerful Magic for Budding Witches | 59

CHAPTER 5   Put It Together and What Have You Got:
Bibbidi-Bobbidi-Choose | 81

PART TWO HAPPILY EVER AFTER . . . 87

CHAPTER 6   You Can Be Your Hero, Baby | 89

CHAPTER 7   What to Expect When You're Expecting
(Certain Things from Your Relationship) | 99

CHAPTER 8   When You're a Prince, They Let You Get Away
with Anything | 115

CHAPTER 9   Save the Drama for Your (Fairy) God-Momma! | 127

CHAPTER 10 Spinning Shit into Gold | 143

CHAPTER 11 Happily Ever After It's Over | 161

CHAPTER 12 True Self-Love Conquers All | 183

Conclusion: Cinderella, a Transformation | 187
Notes | 197
Further Reading | 203
Acknowledgments | 205
About the Authors | 208

INTRODUCTION
FAIRY-TALE FUCKED

HELLO, SHANNON AND BEAU HERE. We're so glad you've picked up our book. Maybe you did so because you liked the title. No judgment; we like the title too. (Confession: sometimes we choose a bottle of wine because we like how pretty the label is.)

Cinderella, You Bitch is a title we've been joking about for years, while living through the ups and downs of romance, holding partners to impossible expectations, and clutching fast to our childhood dreams of finding true love. At some point—neither of us can remember when— the idea that we could never be complete without our soulmate began to feel like a joke, one in which we had become the punchline. So, we began examining our own beliefs more carefully. For instance, why the fuck were we basing our ideas about love on ridiculous fairy-tale notions like love at first sight? (We wasted a lot of years waiting to lock eyes with some random on the train and just *know*.) And why did we believe that our lives would radically change for the better the moment we found "The One"?

We didn't know it at the time, but these questions were about to launch us onto a path of self-discovery that we'd travel for years, and would ultimately lead to the creation of *Cinderella, You Bitch*.

Now, a quick shout-out to those of you who picked up the book because you *didn't* like the title. Maybe you were all like, "Wait a minute! Why are you picking on my girl Cindy? What did she ever do besides bring joy to millions of children by representing hope, perseverance, and love—all while keeping a spotless house? What's your problem with princesses?"

Well, three things.

First, we have problems with princes too, so no worries.

Second, it's totally fine if you love Cinderella, but . . .

Third, and this one may come as a shock: Cinderella isn't a real person. She's a concept. A construct. And a deeply flawed one at that.

Doesn't it seem strange to you that Cinderella had to appear rich, thin, and beautiful to get Prince Charming's attention? Also, he falls in love with her in an hour? Girl must have had her lashes on. Why else would he need to use her shoe to find her again? Dude couldn't recognize her without her makeup.

This story is dangerous. How so, you ask? Let's answer that with a little story of our own.

∽◦∾

Once upon a time, in a land not so far away, there lived a smart, successful, strong woman. At work she was a #BossBitch, and outside of work she was surrounded by a circle of supportive, like-minded friends. Money? Let's just say, the shoes on her feet—she bought 'em; the clothes she was wearing—she bought 'em. Not to mention her vacays in the sun—yeah, she bought them too. So, of course, she was perfectly happy, right?

Wrong.

'Cause when our heroine looked in the mirror, she didn't see the kick-ass independent woman everyone else did; she only saw a sad-sack singleton. She'd stare at her reflection and think to herself: *Why am I all alone? Why can't I find true love? If only there was someone to sweep me off my feet, to be my everything, then my life would be complete. But I'll never be enough* . . .

Skkkkkrrrrrt!

We interrupt this story for an important observation:

Molly, you in danger, girl.

Not that we blame her. She's clearly suffering from what we call Cinderella Syndrome. And she's not alone. Cinderella Syndrome is pervasive in North American culture and affects almost everyone to some degree. At its most basic, Cinderella Syndrome is a by-product of the most toxic fairy-tale fantasies that have wormed their way into our collective culture as "truth." We're talking about the idea that the key to happiness is only found in romantic love and that there is only one person out there who will be your everything.

But wait, there's more!

We're also talking about the fantasy that this once-in-a-lifetime true love of yours will be so smitten with your perfection that he would die for you! And he will never, ever, let you down. And yes, we said "he" because that's part of the fairy-tale fantasy too: the story of true love can only look like the expression of heteronormative monogamy that culminates in marriage. The end.

And while we aren't here to dispute the beauty, magic, and joy that can come from finding someone special, we *are* here to say that this fairy tale is making everyone sick. Even us.

We both suffered from Cinderella Syndrome, but its symptoms manifested very differently for each of us.

Let's start with Shannon.

Hi. Shannon here. I've always been in love with the fantasy of love. I was lucky. I experienced plenty of love as a child from my parents, but what I'm talking about is love from a romantic partner. I desperately wanted someone who desired me, was inspired by me, and would make any sacrifice to keep me because they would be lost without me. In short, I wanted to be the center of someone's absolute adoration because I thought that was the pinnacle of love. (Pedestal, anyone?) I grew up seeing women being admired and rescued by men on film, and I wanted that IRL. It never occurred to me that love could offer something so much deeper, richer, and more profound.

As a result, I chose men who weren't the right fit for me because I was sure I would win them over and make them love me (just like Cinderella did in that pretty little dress with those nice glass slippers), and that then they'd be sure to see how lucky they were to have me and I'd feel fulfilled.

It didn't turn out well.

I married an artist and wanted to be his muse throughout our happily ever after. (We got divorced.) I fell for an author and thought I would be the person with whom he could have the deepest, most profound conversations. Turned out he just wasn't that into me. Over and over again it felt like my dream of true love conquering all just kept slipping through my fingers. Really, though, I just didn't understand love at all. At least until the day I took that step back to examine the fantasy that had been driving my love life. That's when I began to realize that the validation I desired needed to come from within before I could be truly open to real, healthy love, and that the praise and adoration I was seeking was not a strength but a weakness, one that was preventing me from finding true connection. Truthfully, it took forty-three years, lots of therapy, and many, many real-talk sessions with Beau for me to start to recognize my patterns, identify the beliefs driving my behavior, and understand that I was chasing an out-of-control story with some pretty unrealistic expectations—a story that was holding me back from finding happiness in my relationships. Most important, I came to understand that the real source of true love was internal, not external.

I am now on a journey of understanding and loving myself first (full disclosure: it's something I'm still working on and will be for the rest of my life), so that whenever I choose to bring someone else into my land far, far away, you best believe it's magic.

Now we have Beau. If I had a microphone, I'd say something cheesy like "Take it away," but, well, you get the idea. So, without further ado . . .

Hi, I'm Beau. Growing up gay in the eighties and nineties in a small religious town in Alberta, Canada, was a really freeing and nurturing experience. No, wait, it was the opposite of that: it fucking sucked. The Cinderella narrative was pretty much the *only* story available to me when it came to dreaming about my future. We were all supposed to find the one person God had created for us, get married (no sex first or off to Hades for you), have kids, and all live happily ever after. Not only was it heteronormative and incredibly banal, it was utterly outside my grasp.

Unlike Shannon, I didn't grow up chasing the fairy tale, because I knew I could never have it. I was locked out of the kingdom—the one where only some people (and certainly not gay people) could love who they love and be loved by God.

When I realized that the only narrative for a happy life wasn't one that was available to me, I started to make up my own story—and it was the opposite of a fairy tale. It went something like: *I'm not allowed to be happy. I won't ever find love. If I want kids, I can't have them. All the things that are possible for "normal" people are never going to happen for me. There must be something wrong with me. God doesn't love me, and neither will anyone else.*

For years, I felt like I didn't have the right to choose the person I wanted to love, and I felt very suspicious of anyone who claimed to love me. "Harmless" stories such as Cinderella's do incredible damage to those they fail to represent. It took me a long time to stop focusing on the fact that I was on the outside of the kingdom looking in and realize that I didn't want to be inside those gates in the first place.

Like Shannon, I credit our years of friendship, candor, and support as pivotal to helping me step away from the bondage of the fairy-tale fantasy and into the freedom of living and loving exactly as I choose. Now, after years of working on myself and creating positive change in the way I view myself and others, I am able to communicate better and be more authentic with others, and I'm no longer afraid to express what I need. I know exactly what I want in a partner and how I want to be in a relationship. Operating from this place of clarity and choice has changed my life and relationships forever.

So, there you have it. Our own sad Cinderella Syndrome stories. You'll notice that they are quite different from one another. That's because Cinderella Syndrome can manifest in many different ways. Luckily, the symptoms are pretty easy to spot.

You may be suffering from Cinderella Syndrome if you have ever exhibited any of the following:

- You think you'll feel whole/complete/worthwhile, etc., after you meet the person you are supposed to be with.
  In our experience, relationships draw attention to and make us face our deficiencies; they don't cure them.

- You want to be rescued in some way. Preferably by a sexy doctor or a slightly sadistic self-made billionaire à la *Fifty Shades of Grey*.
  Rescue relationships start off with a power imbalance that never rights itself. At a certain point you are probably going to get sick of being infantilized. (Unless that's your kink.)

- You think love can solve all problems.
  Love is great, honey, but it ain't no magic spell.

- You NEED a relationship to be happy.
  Well, sure, it doesn't hurt to have someone to share things with, but NEED is a pretty strong word. What would life be like if you didn't need a relationship but instead chose to have one?

- You believe that having to work at communication with someone means they can't possibly be "The One."
  Unless your significant other is a psychic, this shouldn't be a thing.

- You think that if you don't have mind-blowing, addictive, and constantly amazing sex with someone that you shouldn't pursue a relationship.
  In our experience, that kind of sex, more often than not, happens with people you DEFINITELY shouldn't be in a relationship with!

- You think relationship therapy means the end of a relationship.
  This shit takes growth. And sometimes you need to call in a pro.

- **You think relationships are a 50/50 proposition.**
  We like to say that relationships are 100/100—two whole people coming together and giving the best they can in any moment.

- **You find yourself in the same relationship with different people.**
  Looks like we got ourselves a pattern! More about this later.

- **You think life should be like a romantic comedy.**
  How's that working out for you so far?

- **You're overly committed to only ONE kind of relationship.**
  We LOVE ice cream, but we don't want it to be the only thing we ever eat ... or do we? Hmmm ... let us get back to you on that.

- **You believe your wedding day will be the most important day of your life.**
  "Huzzah," say all the diamond sellers and that guy with his tacky overpriced wedding venue on Long Island. "Maybe spend your money on something else?" say all married couples everywhere.

If you recognize any of these symptoms, have no fear: the freedom you are looking for is right in the pages of this book. We've been working on the cure for years.

We've been dating, loving, losing, and picking ourselves up and trying again for more than two decades. We've had therapy, pursued deeply transformational trainings, ayahuasca journeys, psilocybin weekends, and long, deep cryfests. We've immersed ourselves in relationship research and personal growth practices. We've studied under great teachers. We've meditated (works), used crystals (doesn't work), and, yes, we've read and watched a lot of fairy tales. Are we relationship coaches?

No.

Are we real people who were finally fed up with all of it and deter-mined to try something new?

Abso-fucking-lutely.

That's not to say we won't call in the relationship-coach big guns from time to time in this book. We're all for outside opinions and people who know more than we do. But there's nothing like living through things to make you understand them—and we've lived through a shit-ton.

No doubt, you have too.

That's why we're going to ask you to look deep within yourself. Because unlike what the fairy tales are selling, love doesn't always come around at the perfect time. In fact, it usually comes along when you least expect it. The trick is to know it when you see it—outside of all the lofty expectations we've been subconsciously sold—and then to know what to do with it. This all starts with knowing yourself.

This book will help you uncover your beliefs, identify your own pat-terns, and challenge your behaviors and perceptions when it comes to love and relationships. We're going to be with you step by step as you explore what you actually want in a relationship and why. Then you're going to practice choosing differently for a change.

This is a very noble quest that you're about to embark upon in order to break this wretched curse. We promise we'll try to keep the lame fairy-tale jokes to a minimum (well, minimum-ish) if you promise to start taking a long, hard look at yourself, beginning with your beliefs. So, are you ready to smash your glass slipper and take control of your roman-tic life? Then read on, dear friend. Your very own version of happily ever after is waiting to be written and—spoiler alert—the hero at the end of this tale is YOU.

PART ONE

Once Upon a Time . . .

CHAPTER 1

ONCE UPON A TIME, FAIRY TALES WERE PRETTY GRIMM

HAVE YOU EVER WATCHED *THE LAST UNICORN*? It's an animated film that was released in the early eighties, based on the book of the same name by Peter S. Beagle. It's a story about a beautiful unicorn who, upon learning that she is the last of her kind, leaves the protection of her idyllic forest to learn what has become of the others. She faces many dangers out in the human world; namely, everyone trying to catch her. She's caged for a time by a witch and lands a three-breasted bird for a roommate. (The bird has nothing to do with the main plot but is straight-up awesome, so we *had* to mention it.) Anyway, the unicorn is freed by a friendly magician who then transforms her into a girl so she can travel incognito. She eventually learns that the other unicorns have been rounded up by an evil king who holds them captive, guarded by a sinister red bull. Brave AF, the unicorn-in-girl's-clothing shows up at the king's castle, gets a job as a cook, and spends her nights searching for the red bull. The king's son falls in love with her, tries to fight the red bull for her, and—wait for it—fails. (Don't send a prince to do a unicorn's job, we always say.) She returns to her true form, defeats the bull with her unicorn realness, and frees all her unicorn friends. The prince is all, "Stay with me forever, I love you," and she's like, "I love you too, but sorry, I'm a unicorn, so buh-bye," and hoofs it back to her forest.

Fucking amazing, right?

The Last Unicorn grossed $6,455,330 at the box office worldwide. The animated version of *Cinderella*, by comparison, grossed $263,591,415 worldwide. Think about that. *Cinderella*—a story about a girl with zero agency who's basically a prisoner (albeit a very tidy prisoner) until she gets rescued by a dude—grossed almost *forty-one times more* than a story about a girl who kicks ass and is secretly a unicorn! Oh, and we should add that the live-action version of *Cinderella*, which was released in 2015, didn't fair too badly either. It grossed $534,551,353 in worldwide release.

We think this is a shame. The stories we absorb as children have a profound impact on our sense of the world and our place in it. Why? Because stories are powerful, primal, and, at their essence, each contains a seed—a little morality lesson planted into the mind of the reader that may eventually bloom into a belief.

The history of storytelling is as old as civilization. Back when our ancestors were painting on cave walls, they were doing what we now do daily without even thinking about it—minus the face-flattering filters. According to Lisa Cron, author of *Wired for Story: The Writer's Guide to Using Brain Science to Hook Readers from the Very First Sentence*, "Story was crucial to our evolution—more so than opposable thumbs. Opposable thumbs let us hang on; story told us what to hang on to."

In other words, we Homo sapiens don't just dig stories, we *need* them. They help us make sense of the world; create a sense of order out of chaos; and feel safe, connected, and in control. They also teach us lessons, and not always valuable ones. Which makes a pretty compelling argument for critically examining our shared stories that target children during their formative years of development.

Yes, fairy tales, we're looking at you.

Ready for a history lesson? Don't worry, there'll be games!

CINDERELLA IS *HOW* OLD?

Fairy tales are stories with a bit of magic built in. Even the word *fairy* implies that these tales have been brought to us by some mythical creature with the power to protect us, or to make our wishes come true with the wave of a wand.

There's much debate about where the first popular fairy tales originated, as their oral history long predates the invention of the printing press in the fifteenth century. For the purposes of this chapter, we'll stick to written fairy tales, which narrows our focus to four dead white dudes: Giambattista Basile, Charles Perrault, and Jacob Ludwig Karl Grimm and Wilhelm Carl Grimm (the Brothers Grimm). They are not the only authors of fairy tales, but they are responsible for popularizing most of the fairy tales we know best. Actually, they weren't *really* the authors of these tales. As we mentioned, with the invention of the printing press, folk tales that had long been passed down orally were able to be written down and mass produced. This marked a new dawn in storytelling (a.k.a. mass hypnosis). Everyone started reading the same things. Books would have been the movies of the day, but with only a tiny handful of studios producing them, the selection was pretty bleak. (Diversity of voices and thought? Forget it.) When it comes to Cinderella, she was in the mix right from the beginning. Girl's been around for more than six hundred years, although she's gotten quite a bit of work done.

Giambattista Basile (1576–1632) is widely credited for penning the first modern literary version of the Cinderella story with his tale *The Cat Cinderella*. In Basile's version, Cinderella was named Zezolla, had two stepmothers, and wasn't exactly the milquetoast maiden we know today. She loathed her first stepmother and confided to her governess that she wished *she* was her mother. So, the sly governess encouraged Zezolla to "accidentally" drop the lid of a heavy trunk on the neck of her step-mother. The next time Stepmommy Dearest was rooting around in the chest for a dress, Zezo pulled the ol' "and I oop . . ."

One evil stepmother down.

Zezolla then convinced her father to marry the governess. Cue the Rise of the Evil Stepmother: The Sequel. Unbeknownst to Zezolla or Daddy, the widowed governess had six daughters from a former marriage, and our heroine ended up being neglected and treated even worse than before. The stepsisters didn't even call her by her real name but instead called her "Cat Cinderella," relegating her to the status of an animal.

Cat Cinderella was forced to live her life as a servant, until the deliv-ery of a magical date tree that grew a fairy. The fairy taught Cat a magic spell which, when chanted, gave her a total makeover better than any-thing you'd see on *Queer Eye*. She took her new and improved self to feast day and met the king. The king, transfixed, sent a servant to stalk her (because, true love), and ultimately Zezolla became his bride.

And they all lived happily ever after.

Wasn't that a lovely tale?

And now, just as we promised, we are going to take a break from our history lesson to play a little game we like to call Name That Narrative.

If stories are morality lessons dressed up as entertainment (the better to brainwash you with, my dear), then what can we learn from *The Cat Cinderella*?

While we don't condone murder by trunk, we appreciate that this Cinderella had at least a touch of agency, although it only ended up making her life worse. So, perhaps this is a cautionary tale for young girls? A way to encourage them to save their social-climbing skills for the art of marriage over murder? There also seems to be a strong message that you can never trust older women because they are all just looking out for themselves. Also, makeovers lead to love, men get whatever they want, and the girl considers herself lucky.

That was fun. Let's try another.

We'll look at one more of Giambattista's fairy tales before moving on. Let's try *Sleeping Beauty*.

In his version, Sleeping Beauty was named Talia and, in similar fashion to the tale we know, was pricked by a splinter and fell into a coma. She was then locked up in an estate and abandoned, only to be discovered by an adventurous king who found her so beautiful he just had to have her. To be fair, he *tried* to wake her up, but in the end, he decided he'd just rape her while she was sleeping. Talia became pregnant, gave birth to twins, and managed to nurse them—all while fast asleep. (Some fairies provided a bit of assistance to the unconscious mother, prompting us to ask . . . um, where were they when she was getting raped?) Talia finally woke up when one of her children sucked the splinter out of her finger (but not when her kids were gnawing her nipples off). When the royal baby daddy returned for a little conjugal visit, he found Mom awake and—you guessed it—she fell in love with him.

And they all lived happily ever after.

Okay, raise your hand if you're seriously all-the-way creeped out.

Our hands are up. Way up. And if we were playing Name That Narrative, we might say something about how Giambattista likes his women chaste, passive, and powerless and his men powerful, proactive, and not even a little bit accountable. We're done with Giam. Let's move along to dead white guy number two: Charles Perrault.

Seventy-three years after *The Cat Cinderella*, Charles Perrault (1628–1703) released his version of the Cinderella story, called *The Little Glass Slipper*. His version is most similar to the one we know today, with just a few modifications. Like, his Cinderella's name was actually Cinderwench, but the youngest stepsister, being generous of heart, called her Cinderella. Also, the mice weren't her friends; she fetched them from a live trap when her fairy godmother was casting around for the carriage crew. A rat and several lizards from the garden were thrown into the mix as well.

The biggest difference, however, is the ending. In Perrault's version, Cinderwench—because she's *so* ridiculously nice (or maybe because she suffered from a touch of Stockholm syndrome)—brought her bitch stepsisters with her when she moved into the castle and set them up with some lords. And we don't even have to play Name That Narrative with this one, because Perrault literally spells it out for us. Instead of writing "The End," he writes, "Moral: Young women, in winning of a heart, graciousness is more important than a beautiful hairdo."

We notice he didn't bother to address young men, or any men, for that matter. Perhaps he also should have added: "Moral: Morals are for women."

Perrault, the original mansplainer, was consistently generous with providing moral interpretations at the end of his stories for his feeble-minded readers. His version of *Little Red Riding Hood*—which is essentially a cautionary tale about the dangers of trusting men—ends with Little Red Riding Hood getting into bed with the wolf and being eaten alive. Once again, he makes sure the narrative lesson is clear. "Moral: Children, especially attractive, well bred [*sic*] young ladies, should never talk to strangers," Perrault writes. "Watch out if you haven't learned that tame wolves / Are the most dangerous of all."

He forgot: "Moral: If Little Red Riding Hood had stuck to less flashy clothing, she wouldn't have attracted the wolf's attention in the first place." (Just saying.)

No history lesson on Cinderella would be complete without mentioning the rock stars of fairy tales: the Brothers Grimm. Jacob Ludwig Karl Grimm (1785–1863) and Wilhelm Carl Grimm (1786–1859) are credited with popularizing many of the fairy tales we know today. They collected the various versions of popular German and European folk tales of Perrault and Basile and made smash hits out of *The Frog Prince*, *Beauty and the Beast*, *Snow White*, and *Little Red Riding Hood*, to name a few. Their collection was published in 1812, with eighty-six folk tales included. This early edition didn't sit so well with children, as it was considered too gruesome, so modifications were made. By the twentieth century, their collection was the second most popular book in Germany. (The Bible took top spot, if you're wondering.)

The Brothers Grimm told the story of Cinderella as well, but they made a few modifications of their own. Instead of having a fairy god-mother, Cinderella is prettied up with the help of birds and forest creatures. When she gets to the ball, her forestry frock goes down as a hit, and the prince does his thing—falls in love, finds the slipper, searches the countryside . . . yadda yadda . . . until he finally arrives at Cinderella's door. Now, this is where the Grimms get a little, well, grim. Cinderella's stepsisters are both determined to be the prince's bride. Their mother, seeking to encourage them, suggests they cut off pieces of themselves (a toe on one, a heel on the other) to try to make the shoe fit. Their mother is so invested in their self-mutilation that she actually runs and fetches the knife for them. Sadly, their bloodshed is for naught. Ultimately, the prince finds his true love, and the stepsisters begrudgingly attend the wedding, where they are attacked by pigeons who peck out their eyes and leave them blind.

And they all lived happily ever . . . never mind.

Since the Brothers Grimm didn't feel the need to include a morality statement at the end of their story, we'd love to take a crack.

All of the women in this story were desperate to be the right fit for the prince after only a few minutes of interaction with him. But what do we really know about this guy? He could be a sociopath, a total mama's boy, have a baby carrot for a dick, or maybe he's just hella boring. We don't know and neither did they! But every woman in the room seemed to have some pretty strong ideas about what it would mean to be chosen by him. Even the stepmother is so eager for his approval that she coerces her daughters into mutilating themselves.

Have you ever cut off pieces of yourself to be the right fit for someone else? Or tried to mold and shape yourself into what you think someone wants you to be? We have, and looking back at those times, we can see it happened because we didn't know how great we were back then. The fact is, none of the women in this story choose themselves. Instead, they are all waiting for someone to choose them. And leading the pack is our poster girl for passivity—Cinderella.

In all three versions of this story, Cinderella is consistently portrayed as having zero agency or power to choose a different path for herself—sans murder, anyway. It's only once she appears privileged and beautiful that her luck begins to change. Cue our collective female obsession with being pretty, thin, and rich. And, of course, once a rich and powerful man falls in love with her, she is saved. All of this toxic nonsense is dressed up as a beautiful love story where the prince is so enchanted by Cinderella and her beauty that he simply has to have her. You know who else just "had to have" people they saw only once? The guy from *Silence of the Lambs*. "It rubs the lotion on its skin or else it gets the hose again!"

Another interesting facet of these tales is that in two out of three versions, an older woman is there to guide Cinderella, for better or for worse. Whether it's a governess convincing her to put a lid on Evil Stepmom the First, or a fairy godmother casting spells to make her more beautiful and get her off to the ball, these older women don't seem to be that much more progressive in their thinking than Cinderella. They just end up reinforcing the idea that the prince is the answer to all her problems. If any of these stories had been written by a woman, we might have seen a more positive representation of older women, especially when it comes to empowering the younger women around them. But as we said before, stories are powerful. Men were keen to hold on to these reins for as long as possible, so it would be many more years before women authors were allowed anywhere near the printing press (unless they were cleaning it).

CONTEXT IS EVERYTHING

Now that you're up to speed on your History of Cinderella, we'd like to take a moment to go a little deeper into the cultural context that drove Cinderella's mass popularity. Around the same time as the Grimms' first publication, Romanticism was taking hold across Europe. A reaction against the Enlightenment, Romanticism basically turned everyone into drama queens. Order, calm, harmony, balance—begone! These boring qualities were all rejected by Romanticism in favor of the irrational, the imaginative, the spontaneous, and the emotional. People started appreciating nature more and considered emotion higher than reason, and everyone (everyone!) became preoccupied with the idea of the hero.

When you put Romanticism and fairy tales together, what have you got? Some pretty substantial shifts concerning ideas about love and relationships. Remember how we used to keep our peepers peeled on the train for the magical eye-lock that would signal we'd found our soulmates? Well, that whole idea is ripped straight out of the Romanticism playbook.

Author and philosopher Alain de Botton addressed the concept of Romanticism and how we think about love and soulmates in his "On Love" talk at the Sydney Opera House in 2016. According to de Botton, "The Romantics are very keen on the notion of happily ever after. That love is not just a passing phase, it is forever." However, de Botton also points out that in Romantic literature, lovers typically die quite young and are also very keen on suicide and dramatic endings. He goes on to say that according to Romanticism, you are supposed to see your beloved and just *feel* they're the person for you because love is based on instinct.

The ideal meeting for romantics would take place in some sort of gorgeous natural setting like, say, a rainbow-hued waterfall, or while watching a magnificent sunset. Right after tripping over your petticoat or losing consciousness because your corset is too tight, a dashing gentleman would appear as if from nowhere to catch you in his muscular yet genteel arms, and you'd know immediately that he was your soulmate.

To sum up: if it's dramatic, emotional, completely ridiculous, and obviously predestined, then you've found your true love!

Romanticism eventually gave way to Realism, and then Naturalism, and then Modernism, and then Who-Cares-ism, but some of its ideals are still kicking around Western culture to this day—most notably, Romanticism's preposterous notions about love and gender. Now, we are aware that we're making some sweeping generalizations here, but think about it: Has anything really changed since Romanticism when it comes to how we view love? Aren't we all, in some way, living with the idea of finding that one perfect person? Aren't we hoping we'll meet them in some wildly romantic way? Or that sparks will fly out of our eyeballs when we look at each other? Compound this with the assertion that good girls like Cinderella can't ask for what they want but have to wait for it, and you've got a big mess: so many of us still pining away for that great guy, hoping he'll choose us, or come back to us, or bring us a matching pair of shoes.

We have Disney to thank for our most modern iterations of the Cinderella story. Just like written fairy tales, Disney's animated movies are intended for children. They are big-screen, highly immersive, emotional events, and the impact is quite profound for young viewers. Especially considering that almost every story begins with the loss of a parent (or parents). Have you noticed that?

Mark Groves, human connection specialist and all-around awesome human, pointed this out to us when we sat down to chat with him about relationships (good stuff from that interview coming to you in part two).

Cinderella? Abandoned. Snow White? Abandoned. Bambi? Yep, you guessed it. There's always the death of the mother or father. Or both. Even *Frozen*, which does its best to change the wait-to-be-rescued narrative, leaves Elsa and Anna alone to fend for themselves. Moral: Disney likes its women young and vulnerable.

It's also worth mentioning that Disney had its cultural rise in the postwar era, when American society doubled down on exalting traditional (subservient) roles for women as men came home from war. Rosie the Riveter was out, Suzy Homemaker was in. And Disney's princess stories were feeding the flames of all those rekindled home fires and raising the next generation of girls to desire this exact same thing.

Beau here. How old were you when you watched your first princess movie? I was just four when I saw *Snow White* in the theater. It was the first movie I had ever been to, and I remember it vividly; in fact, it may be one of my earliest memories. The smell of the popcorn; the dark rust-colored fold-down seats; the hard, sticky concrete floor. I even remember where I sat. I remember being terrified of the evil queen, fascinated by the cartoon landscapes, and enchanted by Dopey's cute little mug. But the fairest of them all was Snow White. Beautiful, young, willow thin, and, well, white—*everyone*, including the gorgeous, powerful queen, was obsessed with her. I remember the intensity of my relief when the prince saved her and my joy when he made her his bride. But I left that theater that day with a brand-new anxiety—and the beginning inklings of shame. Did I want to be rescued by a handsome prince? Or did I want to be one? Or both?

Shannon here. My first movie memory is very different from Beau's. The first film I remember seeing was *Legend*, starring a pre-Hollywood-makeover snaggletoothed and unibrowed Tom Cruise as the hero (Jack). The villain—the Lord of Darkness—was played by a curiously sexy and very horny (literally; he has huge horns) Tim Curry. There was a princess too (natch), named Lili and played by Mia Sara. The entire premise revolved around capturing and rescuing unicorns. Yes, unicorns again. Cut me some slack; I was eight and unicorns were my thing.

Legend has a different plotline than your average fairy tale because the story begins with Jack and Lili already in love. The meddling Lord of Darkness, seeking to plunge the world into eternal, well, darkness (cut him some slack; darkness was his thing), captures a pair of unicorns and Lili as well. He cuts off the stallion unicorn's horn for its power and then tries to make Lili his bride. (The Dick of Darkness might be a better name for him.) Fortunately, Lili is strong and sets boundaries early, telling Darkness she prefers to stand when he asks her to sit. Trope twist! When he offers her his heart and soul (wait, can the devil even have a soul?), Lili plays him so she can gain access to the unicorn mare and sets her free. Despite all her agency, Lili still falls into a classic maiden coma and needs to be rescued by true love's kiss. (Calling Mr. Cruise to the set.) She is saved, the stallion unicorn is saved and reunited with his mare (yes, the unicorns get a love story too), and Jack and Lili run off into the sunset—literally.

Okay. A few things here. One, that movie was outrageously scary for an eight-year-old. I had nightmares for weeks. But beyond that, I picked up a few other things—namely, that love will conquer all, boys will always need to save you (even when you're strong and can stand up to the devil), and Tom Cruise looks cute as a forest boy—snaggletooth and all.

Today, modern retellings of the Cinderella story are everywhere. From *Pretty Woman*, where Cinderella is recast as a down-on-her-luck sex worker, to *Fifty Shades of Grey*, where Anastasia must submit entirely to the rich, handsome savior who swoops in to "rescue" her, proclaiming that he doesn't "do" relationships. (He does end up changing for her, but that's how we know it's a fairy tale.)

Once you really start to look around, you'll see that the fairy-tale fantasy has gotten its big bad teeth into every nook and cranny of our collective storytelling. It's on TV and in the cinemas (and we're not just talking rom-coms either!). It's sold to us by Hinge, which proudly proclaims that it's an app "designed to be deleted"—because true love can definitely be found by swiping right. America's top music hits are dealing in little else. Did you know that LeAnn Rimes' version of "How Do I Live?" set a record for staying on the Billboard Hot 100 chart for sixty-nine weeks until it was toppled by Jason Mraz with his song "I'm Yours" (another codependency nightmare in disguise)? Have you ever read the lyrics to "How Do I Live?" They pine about what would happen if the love of the singer's life were to up and leave. There's talk of not being able to breathe (Does she die?); about there being no sun in the sky (Really? The apocalypse came because your partner left you?); about the world pretty much disappearing.

It goes on. We won't. You guys, this is *all kinds* of wrong.

We're not saying you can't enjoy this song, or sing it to yourself in the shower if you're going through a tough breakup. Have at 'er. We know that in our younger days (okay, in our older days too) we definitely threw ourselves onto our beds, in ultimate drama-queen style, after some asshole broke our fragile hearts. And we most definitely listened to that damn song on repeat while we wallowed in the great romantic tragedy that our lives had become. But guess what? It was totally counterproductive and caused us way more pain than necessary, and we *did* live without him!

Now what was his name again?

All of these stories are *fantasies*. They are modern-day fairy tales. And in this day and age, stories are hotter than ever. We are immersed in stories all day, every day. Hell, we even watch "stories" on social media. These are fantasies too. If you've ever posted a filtered photo to glam up your life into something that looks better than it really is, then you already know how stories can be used to manipulate the truth. The problem is that these toxic stories about love, acceptance, and happiness are now so ubiquitous and unrelenting that we hardly even notice them anymore. But we need to open our eyes and take a good look around. It's the first step in breaking free from the fairy-tale fantasy that is ruining so many of our relationships.

Once you start to notice all the stories that are being told to you, you are ready for the next step: listening to the stories you are telling yourself. When we are young, we are shaped by the stories we are told. As we get older, we become the stories we tell ourselves, but these inner narratives can be even harder to spot than the external ones.

You can start by getting curious about what stories you've been telling yourself about love.

Are you the sad girl who questions everything about herself, wondering what needs to change in order for you to be chosen?

Are you the boy who thinks he's forever destined to have his heart broken?

Maybe you're the one who believes you need to wait for that exact right person to come along, and by doing so, keeps missing all of the great people right in front of you.

Or perhaps you think there is something wrong with you because you don't want a conventional relationship, and that goes against everything you've been taught.

These kinds of questions can evoke pretty powerful emotional responses because they are fueled by our deepest beliefs and desires. These are the uncharted lands that we're heading into next. But don't fear, brave heart. We're going in together.

CHAPTER 2

MIRROR, MIRROR ON THE WALL

WE HAVE THIS FRIEND MICHELLE. Every Sunday, Michelle makes a traditional roast beef dinner—garlic mashed potatoes, Yorkshire pudding, carrots, gravy, the works. Before she seasons the roast, she carefully cuts off both ends of the meat. It's just what she does. One day, Michelle is preparing a roast for her new boyfriend (because the way to the heart is through the stomach and all that). Anyway, her boyfriend witnesses this strange roast-cutting ritual and asks Michelle why she does it that way. She explains that it was the way her mom always did it, but she isn't sure why. Now Michelle's curiosity is piqued, so she calls her mom to ask. Except her mom doesn't know why she does it either, even though she too has been cooking roasts that way for as long as she can remember. So, Michelle and Mom conference in Grandma, and now we're three generations deep into this meaty mystery. When asked about the roast prep, Granny replies, "It's simple. When I was first married, I received a beautiful roasting pan from my mother, but it was a little bit small, so I always had to cut the ends off the roast." Turns out it wasn't a secret to making the best roast you've ever tasted; it was just pure and simple necessity serving as the (grand)mother of invention. Granny's daughter and her daughter's daughter grew up seeing roasts being cooked this way, so they believed this was how roasts are cooked. Any chef will tell you it's not, but these poor women served and ate dry roasts and wasted hundreds of dollars' worth of grade-A beef for generations because they never questioned their belief about how to cook a decent roast.

In the previous chapter, we examined our collective fairy-tale narrative, but now it's time to turn inward and take a look at the fairy tales we tell ourselves about relationships and love. These are the stories generated by our beliefs, and our beliefs are responsible for pretty much every result we generate in our lives. And you best believe your beliefs will butcher a relationship as easily as Michelle's did her roast.

If we want to change our relationship results, it all begins with a good hard look in the mirror. And instead of just demanding that it show us what we *want* to see—like a certain evil queen we know—we are going to get curious about who we really are. And we're going to start with our beliefs. Self-identity is largely rooted in beliefs: who you think you are; why you act and react the way you do; why you click with someone and why you don't. We are under the spell of our beliefs. But we don't have to be.

So let's get started on breaking this wretched curse.

YOU ARE WHAT YOU BELIEVE

When it comes to beliefs, the most important thing to remember is this: *Beliefs drive thoughts. Thoughts drive feelings. Feelings drive actions.*

We will come back to this concept many times, so feel free to memorize it now if you wish.

Actions are important because they drive your results in life. What this means, at its simplest, is that you are responsible for generating all of the relationship results in your life.

All. Of. Them.

If this sounds like bad news to you, then let us tell you the good news: you have the power to change these results!

Let's say you have a propensity to view yourself as a victim from time to time. Cinderella certainly did. She believed she was the victim of a cruel stepmother and a wicked pair of stepsisters, and that it was her fate to be a poor peasant girl with mice for BFFs. She truly thought that nothing short of magic could release her from her situation. She didn't run away. She didn't fight back. She simply resigned herself to playing the perfect victim. This was her belief, and it became her identity.

Now, don't get it twisted. We aren't the kind of people who enjoy finger-pointing and playing the "blame the victim" game. We aren't interested in blaming others at all; we are *only* interested in looking at our personal narratives that may include instances of victimhood. And we are asking you to gently do the same for yourself, because a great deal of freedom is available to you if you are just willing to consider the idea that you may be playing the victim in certain aspects of your life.

There's nothing to be ashamed of. We all play the victim from time to time. It is a part of being human—mainly because the ego is a tricky bitch who just loves a good victim narrative.

If you want to get all science-y about it, beliefs are associated with the ventromedial prefrontal cortex—the part of the brain involved in self-representation. Do not doubt the power of this part of your noggin'. Playing the victim provides a very safe sense of self, one where you never have to own up to your own problems (and your power to solve them).

How many friends do you have who complain about the many bad dates they've been on and how awful dating is in their city? We have friends around the globe, and you know what? By their accounts, dating sucks in every single city in the world. All of these friends feel they are victims of a poor dating pool. (It's not me; it's my city.) And, by the way, every time you tell yourself—and anyone who will listen to you—about how bad your dating life is, you continue to perpetuate the cycle. That's because you're handing your ego the evidence it needs to reinforce this belief. You believe something to be bad and, guess what? It will never get better.

You are generating these results.

What you focus on, you get more of.

You are what you believe.

DATA DISTORTION AND LIMITING BELIEFS

The situation we've described above is what's known as data distortion or confirmation bias, and you guys, this is real. A data distortion happens when, without even knowing it, you create opportunities for your beliefs to be confirmed at the same time you're turning a blind eye to every instance when those beliefs are disproven.

Let's get back to our friends who perpetually complain about how bad dating is in their city. Well, we have one friend in particular: we'll call her Data-Distortion Debbie. Do you know how many dates Debbie has debriefed with us where the guy just didn't cut it because he wasn't wearing the right pair of shoes, or he was in between jobs, or he was too young, or too old, or he smelled like Fancy Feast cat food? Wait. We actually can't forgive that last one. Anyway, there goes Debbie, confirming her belief over and over again that there is simply no one to date in her city. Except there is. There are potential Debbie-dates everywhere! As there are in your city/town/Podunk village. Now sure, there are some real frogs out there, but ask yourself if you might be discounting some pretty decent people just so you can confirm your beliefs. Ask yourself, *Am I in a data distortion?*

> **Beau here.** When I go out, I often find myself complaining to friends about how no one ever really looks at me or hits on me. (I know, *pooooor* me.) But my friends often point out that I *am* getting checked out. It's just that I am so blind to this that my first instinct is to refuse to see it, even though I know my friends don't lie. My data distortion is so strong that I literally cannot readily accept anything that would disrupt this belief. But I'm working on it.

Beliefs driven by data distortions are the toughest ones to change, precisely *because* they are always creating evidence in their own favor. They're like the star state prosecutor presenting situations, people, and experiences to confirm their case—and the verdict always comes in on their side. Just like it does for our poor date-around Debbie.

Data distortions aren't all negative, though. For example, we all know a girl who isn't *that* pretty or gorgeous but somehow manages to haul in men by the truckload. And not just mediocre-looking dudes either. We're talking about that badass belladonna with the unshakable confidence and mysterious magnetism that you just can't seem to wrap your head around. That za-za-zoo she wields doesn't come from magic; it's fueled by a deep-seated belief. She believes she deserves that D. And she gets it. And every time she does, she creates more evidence to back up that belief.

Unfortunately for many of us, when it comes to love and relationships, we are far more likely to be operating from confirmation biases that are limiting us, even if those beliefs bring us pain. In fact, we're so programmed to stick to our beliefs that once we form them, we will literally do *anything* we can to be right about them.

According to our self-actualization hero (and BFF, once he meets us) Eckhart Tolle, author of several books including *The Power of Now* and *A New Earth: Awakening to Your Life's Purpose*, "There is nothing that strengthens the ego more than being right." This means that we subconsciously choose people who will fulfill our data distortions, and continue to put ourselves in situations that will deliver the proof we need to back up these beliefs. If you believe you don't deserve love, you will consistently look for, find, and become involved with people who are emotionally unavailable. With them, you'll never feel fully loved, and, once again, you get to be right. Yay, you! Except, not really.

Maybe at this point you're all like, "Okay! I'm buying what you're selling, so let's get to changing my beliefs already!"

To this we say, "Yes, let's go!" But also, "Not so fast."

Understanding the impact that your beliefs have on your life is the first step to reclaiming your power. Next, you must *identify* your limiting beliefs, and that's easier said than done. According to Dr. Bruce Lipton, cell biologist and epigenetics researcher, "Scientific assessments reveal that the wishes, desires, and aspirations of our creative conscious minds only control cognitive behavior about 5% of the time. Subconscious programs are in control 95% of our lives."

Do you need a moment to take that in? Our subconscious mind owns 95 percent of the shares of our brain! And most of our beliefs are buried deep within, which makes it quite difficult to identify them. But not to worry: we happen to know an excellent place to start.

BEGIN WITH YOUR EARLIEST BELIEFS

The majority of our most formative beliefs are created at a young age. As we wrote earlier, the human mind is essentially a story-making machine, and during childhood this instinct is on hyper-drive.

Dr. Lipton states, "Of the downloaded behaviors acquired before age seven, the vast majority—70% or more—are programs of limitation, disempowerment, and self-sabotage. These programs were acquired from other people, not from ourselves. Again, being subconscious, these programs are occurring without conscious recognition and awareness."

Our young minds must make meaning and order out of the chaos all around, and this is done through creating stories from our experiences and observations. The beliefs we form as children are carried forward into adulthood and, over the years, their roots become deeper, thicker, and harder to dislodge. There's even a psychological term for it: *belief perseverance*. And the longer we have our beliefs around, the more we come to see them as "fact" or "truth," until we don't recognize them as personal beliefs at all.

Beau here. I wanted to share a story about my boyhood beliefs. From the time I was seven years old, I was being bullied relentlessly. Calls of "FAGGOT" followed me wherever I went. My well-meaning mother, wanting to stop the pain, advised me to cease whatever I was doing that drew negative attention to myself. But as far as I could tell, I wasn't doing anything other than being me. And so, my little-boy brain interpreted these events and cooked up some beliefs. They went something like this: *If I show people who I really am, they will hurt me*, and *The essence of who I am will disappoint the people who love me.*

These two childhood beliefs became my greatest adversaries. I went from being outgoing, performative, and kind, to being introverted, moody, and sometimes not very nice. Through a lot of work and commitment, I've found balance, but those beliefs linger, and they are always trying to manifest evidence that they are right. Thankfully, I've had time, practice, awareness, and experience that helps me to sort through when these old beliefs are in play, and now I get to choose to be different than I was when I wasn't conscious of them.

Often, our beliefs about love and relationship are sewn like seeds into our hearts and minds by our parents or the adults who raised us. We witnessed who they loved and how they were loved. We absorbed lessons on how they communicated or didn't, how they resolved conflicts, and how they treated each other. The list goes on. Essentially, our parents or caregivers set the template for how a romantic relationship plays out. Both of us were fortunate to grow up in very stable households, but we still interpreted and then internalized these observations, and, as adults, our subconscious minds relied on this data to inform our romantic relationships.

Shannon here. Growing up, I was taught that in order to be a good and lovable person, I needed to be kind, giving, and compassionate. There's nothing wrong with that. In fact, it's what makes me a loyal and amazing partner. What I didn't learn was how to extend these same qualities to myself. I was taught to be tough. Somewhere along the line, I also picked up the belief that asking for help is a weakness. This led to a delightful cocktail of needing someone else to bestow the love I wouldn't give myself and a total inability to express my needs or accept help when offered. It doesn't take a psych major to guess that this combination of internal beliefs hurt me and those around me. Deeply. It took me many years to tease out the mess of these conflicting childhood beliefs that were wreaking havoc on my love life.

Just like Beau, once I was able to identify these beliefs and recognize them as concepts formed when very young, I was able to bring my adult self to the work of learning how to choose to believe differently.

Now it's your turn. Can you reflect on some of the ways your parents or caregivers modeled love and relationships? Can you identify any of your own beliefs that may have been formed as a result? Don't forget to include those things that you consider "facts" about love. (These things usually serve as waving red flags, indicating spots where deep internal beliefs are buried.)

Remember, go gently when exploring this kind of relational work. Hidden beliefs often want to stay hidden because once they are exposed, you really do have the power to change them. And it can be scary to step into the role of the hero in your own story, especially if you've been waiting for years to be rescued.

CHANGING YOUR BELIEFS

Okay, are you ready to blast through some old beliefs so you can start building some new ones? If you've been paying attention, you now know that everything you generate is coming from you and you alone. Now it's time to get on the fast track to belief overhaul by training your subconscious mind to get what you want (what you really, really want and a zigazig-ah).

It's actually a fairly simple concept, but then again, so is the idea of doing Pilates every day—and yet we still can't seem to make that happen. This shit takes commitment. And the thing you have to commit to first is to challenge your thinking and take some new actions.

Not to be repetitive (though we are going to repeat this a bunch of times), but your beliefs, thoughts, feelings, and actions are all interconnected. This means you don't have to gun for your deeply rooted beliefs that resist change at all costs. As long as you know what belief you are challenging, you can focus on your thinking around that belief and practice some actions to create evidence to disprove it. (Because beliefs *love* evidence . . . don't forget Data-Distortion Debbie!)

Try this little exercise: Pick something that you believe you are not very good at. For your first practice session, you might want to try something with low stakes. Next, try doing that thing, and as you're doing it, free yourself from the thought that you suck at it. Release the thoughts that normally come up and just allow the thing to happen. We'll give you a personal example.

> **Shannon here.** My five-year-old loves to color, but he only wants to color illustrations that have been drawn just for him and to his specifications. The other night he asked me to draw an anglerfish (he's on an underwater-sea-creature kick right at the moment). Now, I believe myself to be probably one of the worst in the world

when it comes to drawing freehand. Like seriously, stick figures are some of my best work. So, when my son asked me to draw an anglerfish, my immediate thought was: *I can't do that.* But I caught that belief-thought exchange and decided to challenge it. (Besides, a five-year-old with a penchant for underwater sea creatures doesn't like to take no for an answer.) So, I changed my thought from *I can't do that* to *I can try that* and looked up some images of anglerfish. And you know what? I drew a damn good one. My son loved it, and I loved that I was able to make him happy and move past my belief that I can't draw. I went on to draw anacondas and penguins. We spent over an hour together drawing and coloring, and I can't wait to do it again. By noticing and changing my thought and just trying a new action, I was able to shift my belief about how much I suck at drawing. And by doing that, I opened up an entirely new way of spending time with my son.

The exercise above may seem very simple, but when you try this for yourself, get ready to experience some profound shifts. In *Breaking the Habit of Being Yourself: How to Lose Your Mind and Create a New One*, Dr. Joe Dispenza writes, "The latest research supports the notion that we have a natural ability to change the brain and body by thought alone, so that it looks biologically like some future event has already happened. Because you can make thought more real than anything else, you can change who you are from brain cell to gene, given the right understanding."

Changing beliefs requires perceptual shifts. When you deliberately engage in trying new activities and learning new skills, you change the biochemistry of the body and the brain, allowing for new perceptions to replace older beliefs. This is not the only perceptual shift taking place, however. When you slow down and notice your thoughts, you can select a different thought—and this, in turn, breaks down old beliefs even further.

Now, perhaps you are thinking, *This is great and all, but how do I actually apply this to my life?*

Well, we found a powerful practice that was outlined by T.S. Sathyanarayana Rao, M.R. Asha, K.S. Jagannatha Rao, and P. Vasudevaraju in their article "The Biochemistry of Belief" in the *Indian Journal of Psychiatry*. "If you are chasing joy and peace all the time everywhere but exclaim exhausted, 'Oh, it's to be found nowhere!', why not change your interpretation of NOWHERE to 'NOW HERE'; just by introducing a gap, you change your awareness—that changes your belief and that changes your biochemistry in an instant!"

Isn't that a nice little life hack? This also works if you are chasing that elusive perfect relationship and finding it NOWHERE. What if it really was NOW HERE? Putting this thinking into practice could be as simple as looking for all the places you do have love in your life, or taking time to be more loving with yourself.

Once you've experimented with some of these methods for disrupting and rewriting a few low-stakes beliefs, you can begin to work the same magic with beliefs around your relational life.

Remember the process:

1. You start by identifying a limiting belief.
2. Begin to notice and change your thoughts around that belief.
3. Finally, you take action to collect evidence to disprove your belief.
4. Repeat. Over and over again. You must commit to the idea that change is possible.

Instead of writing off the guy who didn't wear the best shoes, try giving him a second date, or move past your belief that a woman can't make the first move and DM that cutie you've been following on Instagram.

You may not get a reply to that DM, and you're probably still going to have some shitty dates, but at least you're opening up to the possibility of change. And when you do dare to try something new, don't judge or hold any attachments to these courageous actions. Magic comes into the space created by possibility. Because if you *expect* that reply from the DM, or if you *think* that second date is going to lead to wedding bells, you're fucked if things don't go the way you think they should. This work is about allowing space for the universe to deliver its highest order to you. You may think this is crazy, but this subtle shift will start to yield big change if you keep at it.

Practice, practice, practice.

You may end up having your very own "ta-da" moment: a moment where you see all the magic that is possible within you, a moment where you prove to yourself that you can change your beliefs and, in doing so, fundamentally change the outcomes in your life—no wand required.

THE WIZARD BEHIND THE CURTAIN

Earlier, we mentioned that beliefs prefer to stay hidden. If 95 percent of your beliefs are buried in your subconscious mind, you can't expect to identify all of them easily. Just like the Great and Terrible Oz, your most frightening and influential beliefs will always be the ones hidden behind the curtain.

But how can you be responsible for beliefs you aren't even aware of?

We can help with that.

It's time to step up to the magic mirror once more. Because it turns out that one of the best ways to expose hidden beliefs is also a great bit of fashion advice . . .

CHAPTER 3

PRINCESS, THAT PATTERN DOES NOT LOOK GOOD ON YOU

IF YOU, LIKE US, were raised on a steady diet of fairy tales such as *Cinderella, Snow White,* and *Sleeping Beauty,* you can be forgiven for thinking that passive beauty is the most desirable quality in a young woman and that jealous older "has-been" women are the bane of humanity. This is because these fairy tales share a similar belief system and, as such, exhibit similar patterns. This is what belief systems do—they create patterns. As in stories, so too in life.

We all know someone who moves from job to job or relationship to relationship. They start off great, but over time somehow the same evil boss shows up, or maybe it's a nasty coworker or emotionally distant partner. It's so easy to blame others when things like this happen, but if the common denominator in the situation is *you,* then guess who's generating these results? We know that's not a very pleasant reality to face, but let's remember this isn't about blame—this is about being responsible for your life. There's a big difference. Blame will leave you as lethargic and trapped as Snow White in her glass coffin. Responsibility, on the other hand, is like handing Ms. White a can of Red Bull and a baseball bat. Things are going to get smashed open.

> **Shannon here.** When I was little, I used to go to an after-school daycare run by a wonderful woman named Connie. Connie had a daughter, Liz, and we were fast friends. We played tons of fun games (usually involving Care Bears), and my fuzzy memories from this time are very pleasant. Connie was warm and kind— and terrified of bees. If Liz and I were playing out in the yard and a bee or a wasp came near Connie, she would run scream- ing into the house like her hair was on fire. And my little brain formed the belief that bees = terrifying. To this day, as a grown woman, if a bee, a wasp, or any sort of stinging insect (let's be honest, *any* insect at all) comes near me, I run away squealing. Every. Single. Time.

Patterns in your life are evidence of your belief system at work. So, if you are looking for the deeply hidden but powerfully influential beliefs that are running your life, it's time to look at your patterns.

If you believe being stung by a bee is terrifying, your pattern will be to run away screaming as fast as you can.

If you believe you can't find love, you will run away from any real chance of it as fast as you can because you're stuck in a pattern of belief, thought, and action that is working to reinforce that belief.

Well, sweetheart, it's time to change outfits.

PATTERNS AND THE BRAIN

Remember maps?

We're not talking about the Google kind. No, we mean the good old-fashioned paper variety. The ones where you had to use a scale to determine how many miles you were traveling, and figuring out how long the journey would take involved mathematical equations and the occasional ruler. Back when we were growing up, we used to keep paper maps in the car; they were the only thing stopping the family from driving to Florida instead of California. Of course, we don't use paper maps anymore; instead, we rely on GPS systems that require little to no thinking. Just punch in an address and boom, your phone tells you the quickest and most direct route to your destination.

When it comes to our patterns, we all have a sort of GPS system running in our minds at all times. But this GPS differs a bit from Waze or Google Maps. Instead of finding the fastest route, or an alternative one if there's something you want to avoid (like a car crash or maybe a toxic ex), your brain's GPS always, *always* takes you the same way, using the exact same roads (or neural pathways) to get you to the exact same destination, over and over and over.

The patterns we produce in our lives are the result of this automatic programming that was installed at a very young age and hasn't been updated since. Can you imagine going on a trip using a GPS that was twenty or thirty years out of date? And yet, so many of us let our antiquated childhood programs plot the trajectory of our lives.

International transformational trainer and author Lisa Kalmin refers to this in her book *The Problem Is How You See the Problem*. Kalmin asserts that our entire internal GPS is running on programming from our past, and yet it is guiding our present-day decision-making. Anyone see a problem here?

Take this information and add it to Dr. Bruce Lipton's assertion that
the majority of your daily thinking, being, and acting is determined by the
beliefs you established during your first seven years of life and you'll see
that you've had years and years and years of your internal guidance system
navigating you to the same destination. At the same time, you've been
collecting years and years and years of evidence that this is the only way it
works for you (thus reinforcing your early beliefs). Even during moments
when you may have veered off the predictable course, your automatic internal guidance system was constantly attempting to override you and deliver
you to the same (sometimes undesirable) destination. Put that together
and what have you got? Patterns, patterns, patterns. Now say that three
times fast, cross your fingers, click your heels, and see if they disappear.

No?

Damn. Keep reading.

SPOT THE PATTERNS IN YOUR RELATIONSHIPS

Okay, so we've got you on the lookout for possible patterns in your life.
That's a great start when it comes to finding hidden beliefs. Patterns are
pretty much like a giant X on your treasure map. Spot a pattern and start
digging; you'll find a buried belief down there somewhere. And as you
now know, once you find a belief, you have the power to start making
some changes.

Spotting a pattern in your relationships isn't rocket science. Start by
looking for repetitions. For example:

- Do you date the same kind of person? (We often justify this
  unconscious choice by claiming to have a "type.")
- When you argue, are you having the same kind of fights?

- When your relationships end, is it always for the same reason?
- Do you only fall for someone when they start to pull away?
- Do you feel smothered and trapped when someone is really into you?

If these examples don't resonate with you, there is another easy way to scout out the patterns in your life: Watch your language. There are certain key phrases that indicate a pattern is afoot. Have you ever said the following:

- "Why does this always happen to me?!"
- "I must be cursed because [fill in the blank] keeps occurring."
- "When it comes to my love life, I never/always [fill in the blank]."

Hello! These are your relational patterns—even if they feel like indisputable facts. *Especially* if they feel like indisputable facts. Make a note of the patterns that are coming up for you.

No matter what your relationship pattern is, know this: the pattern won't change until the beliefs behind the pattern changes. But you *can* practice "pattern disruption" in order to shift these beliefs. Read on!

PRACTICE MAKES DIFFERENT

Remember how 95 percent of our thoughts and actions are a result of subconscious beliefs formed during the first seven years of our life? (We hope you do; we reminded you on the previous page!) Well, we're no mathematicians, but we have calculated that this means only 5 percent of our actions are coming from a place of conscious awareness. Patterns stem from subconscious beliefs, which is why we rarely notice our own patterns, even if they may be obvious to everyone around us. The disruption of the automatic nature of your patterns is often the first step to undoing them, and for that, you're going to have to be really, really mindful. And it's going to take practice.

This is how it works.

First, you need to spot your patterns so you can be *aware* of them. This shifts them into the 5 percent of your brain that you actually have some control over.

Check.

Armed with this spanking-new awareness, you'll be able to notice when you are moving into a typical pattern of reaction when an event occurs. Now, instead of just blindly reacting the same way you've always reacted, you can try asking yourself a question: "How can I shift my perspective on this?"

This question alone is often enough of a disruption to your usual way of being to change the entire outcome of the situation. If you need a little extra push, though, you can also ask yourself: "How am I reacting at this moment?"

This second question allows you to step outside of yourself and be a conscious observer of your patterns, which, in turn, will give you a chance to change your typical reaction or decision.

And remember, this is a *practice*. It is not easy to slow down an automatic response and squeeze a question in before you have your typical reaction. That's okay. You're not going to achieve perfection here. Noticing is what matters. And it will get easier over time.

In her article "The 4 Underlying Principles of Changing Your Brain," Tara Swart, neuroscientist and author, writes, "For the brain to rewire itself it requires a sustained practice of a new behavior which will sufficiently challenge the brain to think in a new way. Imagine how difficult it is to learn a new language or take up a new instrument—this is how hard your brain needs to work to stimulate growth and forge new neural pathways."

Just as with your beliefs, you don't need to start with your most problematic or deeply rooted patterns. In fact, it's better to actively work on patterns and beliefs that aren't so threatening to the core of your identity. Start small. And maybe rally some support.

Once upon a not-too-distant time, we decided to tackle together our long-standing aversion to dancing by signing up for a Beyoncé dance class. We were determined to throw our "I can't dance" beliefs out the window and focus on the fitness and fun of shaking our booties one night a week. When we showed up on the first night, we discovered that this class wasn't just going to be grooving to Beyoncé's greatest hits—this was a full-on, choreographed, shake-it-like-the-single-woman-you-are danceathon. It felt more like a tryout for her next video than a novice dance class.

And it was hard. Hard to figure out where to put our arms, how to move our feet, and how to shake our jelly like Queen Bey. What was even harder was ignoring those familiar thoughts that also joined us on the dance floor: *What is the point of this? You're making a fool of yourself! You can't dance—get over it. You're just a bunch of arms and legs wildly flailing about!*

But we were able to notice our thoughts and choose how to react to them, and our reaction was to break the pattern of quitting and just keep going. And you know what? We ended up being pretty good! JK. At one point—and this is no joke—one of us ended up punching our own face. (We'll never tell who.)

The point is, learning something new is hard at first, and we have often found it can give us an actual headache (especially when you sock yourself in the eyeball). But if you can resist automatically slipping into old thoughts, that headache and that hard work is your brain's neural net shifting and expending energy to move toward a new cognitive program. When you are aware of your patterns and set out to deliberately disrupt them, you are literally training your brain, just like you train your body when you work out. Why not add a little booty shake when you try it, just to make it fun?

EVERY EVENT IS A NEUTRAL EVENT

Thus far we've looked at the nature of patterns and their relationship with our subconscious beliefs. We've explored ways to spot our patterns and provided some first steps you can take to challenge them in order to shift some of your deeply rooted beliefs.

But some patterns are not shifted so easily, and some beliefs resist being seen. What we're talking about here are our core beliefs, our deep-down "This is my identity you're messing with, buster, so back off" beliefs. These beliefs have been with us for most of our lives. Subconsciously, we may feel that we don't know who we are without them, so we'll fight tooth and nail to keep them.

It is worth mentioning that the majority of our relational beliefs fall into this category because they were established early in our lives when our survival was literally at stake. Our relational patterns are formed partly to keep us alive. We do this to get our needs met. As a child, you equate your needs being met with love, even if you grow up in a dysfunctional home. Not surprisingly, then, we need a slightly more sophisticated approach when tackling patterns of this nature and the hidden beliefs associated with them.

We're big fans of Byron Katie, creator of a method of self-inquiry known as "The Work" and the renowned author of *Loving What Is*. Katie tells us that "a belief is a thought that we've been attaching to, often for years." Let's meditate on that for a moment. You are in a relationship with your thoughts and beliefs. You're attached to them and can't imagine any other truth for yourself. But what would happen if you started to challenge those beliefs?

Buckle up, buttercup: it's time for a deep exercise.

Find a place where you can sit quietly without interruption, and think about a hidden belief you may have. If you are not sure how to distinguish a hidden belief, go back to the "always/never" sentences we worked on earlier in this chapter. Maybe you came up with something like *I always get cheated on*, or *Whenever I really like someone, they never stick around*. Whatever it is, look for the sentence that is most emotionally loaded for you. That's how you'll know you've hit your target.

Once you find your hidden belief, connect it to the emotion you are experiencing. Naming the emotion is important because you have to understand what you are dealing with here. You may even want to put pen to paper. Again, the key is bringing awareness to the automatic reaction you are experiencing and finding ways to slow it down. By slowing down, you get to look at your thoughts and ask yourself: *Is this thought true?*

Now, move through Byron Katie's four questions from "The Work" in order to process your deeply emotional events and beliefs. When recounting the event or the belief consider:

1. **Is it true?**

   This is a yes or no answer. Don't go any deeper.

2. **Can you absolutely know that it's true?**

   Recount an example of an event when that belief seemed true to you. Are you sure that whenever you really like someone they never stick around? Is this actually how things happened? Again, this is a yes or no answer.

3. **How do you react? What happens when you believe that thought? (We like to ask ourselves: "What am I making up about myself here? And how does it make me feel?")**

   Does the thought that people don't stick around make you feel sad? Lonely? Depressed? Notice where these feelings are located in your body and any physical sensations you are experiencing.

4. **Who would you be without that thought?**

   Who would you be if you weren't sad? If you didn't feel lonely? What would you be doing as that person? How does that person feel?

Byron Katie tells us that "a thought is harmless unless we believe it. It is not our thoughts, but the attachment to our thoughts, that causes suffering. Attaching to a thought means believing that it's true, without inquiring."

Quite simply, if you can begin to detach from the thoughts and beliefs you have, you can begin to see what is true and what is possible for you. You can begin to reframe your beliefs in such a way that you are no longer suffering from them but learning from them.

Beau here. Recently, I had an experience where this technique really came in handy for dealing with a very difficult situation. When I'm not writing this book, I am a fashion and celebrity makeup artist and photographer. I work with loads of high-profile people, but there was one person in particular I had been wanting to work with for my entire career. And then, lo and behold, that day finally arrived. This person I so deeply admired hired me for a gig. It was a professional dream come true! And it was a fucking disaster.

She was a nightmare client, changing her mind at every turn. Work would be praised and approved one moment only to be followed by a very public rejection of that same work the next moment. I was sweating bullets as I attempted to cater to her unpredictable whims. And as I whirled around, I could hear some of my old familiar beliefs start to sing along: *Maybe I actually have no talent and I'm a crap makeup artist? Maybe she thinks I'm a horrible person?* But I kept right on moving, determined to serve this client with the professionalism and care that I bring to every project.

And then she fired me. Suddenly. Brutally. And in a most humiliating fashion.

My immediate reaction was to be totally and completely crushed. I locked myself in the bathroom and I had my twenty-minute cry and moment of despair as my dream spiraled down the drain and I spiraled around with my thoughts of failure, doom, and how my whole career was in the toilet. And the award for Best Actress in a Drama goes to . . .

But here's the thing. I had been spending time trying to notice patterns and automatic thoughts, and I realized I was right in the middle of one of those events! This wasn't the first time I'd had thoughts like this. So, I got down to work, determined to identify the core belief that was driving this nasty pattern.

If I'd allowed my old pattern to play out, I would have been consumed by guilt and shame, and would have followed that with a spiral that could last for weeks. I had just enough presence of mind to decide that this wasn't going to happen—not this time.

I started by taking a deep breath to calm myself down. This allowed me some mental space to consider why I'd reacted the way I did.

Then I worked through Byron Katie's questions. I asked myself: Was this firing really about me? No. It was not. I realized I had decided that this person's opinion mattered more than others', even more than my own. When I asked myself if that belief was true, I realized that it wasn't. I also realized that I'd thought that if this person approved of me then I would feel better about myself (also not true). Then I asked myself: *What happens when I believe that thought, the one where another's approval is what I need to feel better about myself?* And do you know what the ta-da moment was for me? The understanding that needing someone else's approval makes me feel small. I realized that my need for other people's approval had been around for a long time. A very long time. And when I asked myself the follow-up question—"What am I making up that this means about me?"—suddenly there it was, that old core belief that I'd been dragging around since I was that lonely kid who just wanted to be loved for who I was: *I am broken. I am unlovable.*

When I could look at that core belief, laid bare like that, it was obvious that it was fundamentally untrue and had nothing to do with the event that had just transpired. In that moment, I had the power to deliberately choose to no longer be affected by what had just happened (beyond that twenty-minute cryfest). Once I emerged from the haze of my thoughts, I realized that this person had her own issues—issues that had nothing to do with me—and I didn't need to take this personally at all.

So. Who would I be without that thought? With some further contemplation about the situation, I discovered some really great knowledge about myself and the things I wanted and didn't want in my life. I realized that I really didn't want to work *for* people anymore. I wanted more control over my life and my schedule. I wanted to be my own boss. It ended up being a defining moment for me and propelled me to take the steps that would begin the next chapter of my life. And yeah, it still sucked, but it didn't turn into the giant monster it easily could have. And just like that, I changed my pattern.

FIVE MINUTES A DAY KEEPS THE PATTERN AT BAY

Spotting patterns, identifying beliefs, and working on changing them requires a lifelong commitment, but it is one that will fundamentally change the power you have over your entire life—including your relationships.

At this very moment, you are choosing the people who come into your life. You are choosing the people you allow to remain. When this choice happens at a subconscious level, you may end up choosing people to heal or confirm your childhood wounds, or you may choose people who won't trigger you at all, resulting in a passionless union that has no potential for growth. You are always making choices related to your patterns, even if you think you aren't. Since you're choosing anyway, wouldn't you rather that choice be a conscious one?

This is hard work. As you begin, you will want to be honest with yourself, but don't forget to be kind as well. Keep in mind that blame and shame will only serve to turn you back into a Cinderella—a victim to your patterns. Instead, try making peace with your past. This is an all-important step in overcoming the natural resistance to this work.

Sometimes reframing the events of the past and releasing the emotions that are attached to these events will allow space for new growth and a healthier "GPS."

This is a journey of a lifetime, so small steps can bring you a long way. Sometimes all you need is five minutes a day.

Beau again. Throughout my practice of this transformational work, one of the most important things I've observed about my own patterns is the way I react to compliments. In the past, whenever people gave me a heartfelt compliment, or praise of any kind, I physically recoiled. (How many of you out there do that too? I bet it's not just me.) Now, being Canadian, I think I picked up the belief that it's not very polite to self-promote. Couple that with a religious upbringing that promoted humility and it's no wonder I couldn't accept a compliment from anyone. EVER.

But when I dug into it a bit deeper, I realized this wasn't just about accepting praise from other people. This was about accepting *love* from other people, and learning to love myself. Another way this manifested was in my inability to acknowledge my own accomplishments. Over and over again, I'd do a really great job on something or create something incredible, but I'd just move on to the next thing without taking any time to celebrate my own wins. I was failing to occupy space in my own life and to truly enjoy it. And this was rippling out and negatively impacting every area of my life, from professional to personal. I felt like I was a failure even though I clearly wasn't. I felt like I would never be good enough for anyone, professionally or personally.

I decided I was going to make a conscious effort to change this. So, I implemented a five-minute-a-day practice. Every night I take five minutes to review the day and acknowledge what I accomplished, created, said, or did that I feel good about. And then I let myself actually *feel* good about it. Now, this is a bit different from just listing my daily accomplishments. It requires a bit of concentration and practice to move into allowing myself positive feelings, but once I took the time to really embrace this small practice, I began to see big changes.

I began to see a shift in the way that I valued myself, my work, and my time. In turn, that shifted how other people reacted to me, my work, and my time. (I'm not going to lie: I fuck this up constantly, but I don't make a big story about it, I just keep going.) This process takes serious examination, rigorous determination, and a commitment to change that I have to constantly revisit, but over time it's become a habit and a practice that's changed my life for the better.

A PATTERN OF GRATITUDE

As transformative as Beau's ritual may be, it's not magic. It's based on some pretty solid personal-development principles. The laws of the universe are such that what you focus on is what gains momentum, and ultimately what creates the reality in front of you.

This is why gratitude is such a powerful force.

The universe sees everything as neutral, and it delivers what we put our energy toward. If we are grateful for what we have, the universe will keep delivering that to us. We know, we know, it all sounds far too simple and perhaps a bit woo-woo for some of you, but you should really give it a try. What have you got to lose by looking at things with gratitude? It's an excellent pattern to establish in your life.

Patterns are powerful, and they are part of our wiring whether we like it or not. Besides, not all patterns are bad. You may have some very positive patterns in your wardrobe: great friends that you attract;

resilience in the face of challenge. (Hello, 2020? 2021? Remember *that* nightmare?) Good patterns are worth examining too, if only to learn more about the parts of your belief system you want to keep and the parts you want to toss.

Because that's the whole point. Deciding for yourself.

CHAPTER 4

POWERFUL MAGIC FOR BUDDING WITCHES

BY NOW YOU SHOULD HAVE NEW INSIGHT into some of your core beliefs and how they are influencing the outcomes in your life. Congratulations! You're two-thirds of the way to mastering the spell that will break the fairy-tale-fantasy curse that has been wreaking havoc on your relationships.

Remember our favorite formula? Yes, here we go, all together now: *Beliefs drive thoughts, thoughts drive feelings, feelings drive actions.*

So, are you ready to take a deep dive into the bubbling cauldron of your thoughts and feelings?

Let's start with what you already know.

1. You already know that you (and all of us!) are always writing a story in your mind, and that unless you can recognize your particular story, you cannot write a different narrative for yourself.

2. You already know that identifying and observing your inner world is the key to moving from a reactive to an intentional life.
3. You already know that patterns are a key to identifying your beliefs if you are having trouble figuring out what they are.
4. You already know that your thoughts drive your feelings.

This is an impressive list. Go you! By the end of this chapter, you will also know all about how thoughts and feelings work together and how to disrupt this partnership in order to gain control of your inner world and create the life and love you desire.

It's time for a little spell-casting of our own.

BIG BAD THOUGHTS

To begin, let's take a closer look at your thoughts. You may recognize them as the constant chatter in your mind telling you to hurry up and get dressed, or to stop being so damn lazy and get off the couch, or to get your nails done already because that chipped paint is looking cheap AF. Most of your thoughts are useless banter of this nature, swinging around in your head all day long. The Buddhists call this "monkey mind." These chattering thoughts are like background noise in the brain, not really helpful but also not particularly harmful.

Then there are your negative thoughts. Thoughts like *I'll never meet anyone; I'm destined to spend every single Christmas alone;* or *When did my husband turn into my roommate?* These are harmful thoughts because they keep you stuck in your life and your relationships. And it turns out we have a lot of them.

Jason Murdock explored just how many in a *Newsweek* article titled, "Humans Have More than 6,000 Thoughts per Day, Psychologists Discover."

Wow, you might be thinking, *that's a lot of thoughts!* But what if we told you that Murdock went on to explain that 95 percent of our thoughts are the *exact same* thoughts we had the day before?

We know, right?

And it's not only that: on average, a whopping 80 percent of these thoughts are negative.

In other words, the Big Bad Wolf is in our heads. So how can we keep from getting eaten alive? Well, for starters, we need to strip the wolf of its harmless disguise and see it for what it really is—a deadly predator that is *not* your friend (or your grandmother, for that matter).

Negative thoughts operate a lot like negative beliefs—they are more powerful when they're allowed to stay in the shadows. So, let's turn a spotlight on them.

WHAT YOU THINK IS WHAT YOU GET

Have you ever heard the phrase *What you resist persists?*

Law of Attraction practitioners are all about this idea. They believe that many of us are slowing down our growth by focusing on the things we don't want. When we focus on the things we don't want to happen, guess what? They happen.

In their book *The Law of Attraction: The Basics of the Teachings of Abraham,* Esther Hicks and Jerry Hicks, some of our favorite Law of Attraction teachers, write, "The longer you focus upon something, the more powerful it becomes; and the stronger that your point of attraction is to it, the more evidence of it appears in your life experience."

The other day, we shared this quote with a friend who was bemoaning his single status, and he responded, "Hold up! Are they saying that if I'm focusing on the fact that I am single, then I'm just going to stay single?"

"Yup," we answered. "That's *exactly* what they are saying. Instead of focusing on being single, focus on the relationship you want to have."

This holds true for those of us in a relationship as well. We can choose to focus on all the crap in our current relationship, but that just means more of the same will be on the way. Rather than focusing on the problems, consider solutions.

This shift in perspective is subtle but incredibly powerful. It starts with noticing and then disrupting our negative thoughts.

SLOW DOWN AND SWAP YOUR THOUGHTS

If you were paying attention when we talked about disrupting automatic patterns and shifting hidden negative beliefs (and we know you were!), this concept is going to be familiar to you.

Step one in noticing your thoughts is to slooow the fuck down so you can start creating space between you and your thoughts.

Have you ever tried meditating?

We have. What normally happens is that the moment we begin, our minds immediately start thinking about all sorts of crazy shit. *Hey, did I turn off the stove? I wonder if Brenda responded to my email yet. Probably not, she's such a passive-aggressive little . . . oh, right, I'm meditating. How much longer? My pants are cutting into my stomach. Ugh. I have to stop eating tacos every day. Keep this up and I'll die fat and alone. This is so boring. And kinda pointless. I suck at meditating. Is that cat piss I smell? I don't even have cats. I have way too much to do to just be sitting here. What time is it? Oh, I should check out that new taco truck for lunch.*

It's like trying to sit quietly with a sugar-loaded three-year-old.

But with practice, we've learned that the key to meditation is to simply notice our thoughts, release them without judgment, and go back to stillness. For another few seconds anyway.

Meditation really is a great method for noticing our thoughts and slowing them down, and we highly recommend that you experiment with whatever flavor of meditation appeals to you.

Another reason the simple act of meditation can be so powerful is because it also serves as a reminder that *you are not your thoughts*. Every time you are able to step back from your thoughts and observe them, you become aware that they are separate from you. And once you get a little distance between you and your thoughts, you are able to deliberately choose thoughts that serve you better.

This brings us to a little practice we call "thought swapping." Here's an example of how it works.

We're writing this book in the thick of the coronavirus pandemic, and it is *bleak* out there. For the past few months (but seriously, it feels like years), we've been staying home and thinking a lot about how much it sucks to be stuck at home and how this will never, ever end. And since thoughts and feelings are kissing cousins, our negative thoughts generated feelings of sadness, helplessness, anxiety, and dread.

Real productive thinking.

But the unexpected "gift" of the pandemic was that we were forced to slow down. Spending all that time at home caged in with our own thoughts, unable to distract ourselves or run from them, we started to notice how repetitive our negative thoughts were.

So, we made a deliberate choice to try to notice every time we had one of these thoughts and then shift it to something more positive. Instead of repeating, day after day, "I'm stuck at home," we swapped the thought to "I'm safe at home." As small a shift as it was, we instantly noticed that our days felt a little lighter. We suddenly remembered how lucky we were to be healthy and to have a place to feel safe, and what a privilege this was.

Other considerations for our thought swaps included: "I'm locked in with the same people/person and they're driving me crazy," shifting to "I'm so grateful I have someone to touch and share a meal with." Or, on the other side of that coin: "I'm single during the pandemic and dying of loneliness" becoming "I'm thankful I am safe in my own home and not stuck with a toxic person."

Our thought-swapping practice generated better feelings, which made it easier to generate better thoughts. We were able to override the negative-feedback loop and start a positive-feedback loop instead. We noticed a complete shift in our mood, our level of gratefulness, and our optimism that the pandemic won't last forever. (Seriously, though: we really hope that by the time you read this, we are all out of this nightmare and you're enjoying this book on a packed plane to Mexico or the Bahamas or, well, anywhere.)

You can try a thought swap of your own. If you want to practice with one thought in particular, start by paying attention to something that makes you *feel* terrible. Maybe it's how you look. (We recommend that you choose something personal as opposed to something that involves another person when you first start to practice this technique.) For example, if you are a person who stares at the exact same "flaw" every time you look in the mirror, try the following: Pay attention to your self-talk when you look in the mirror (self-talk is the same as thoughts). Take stock of your repetitive thoughts (*My nose looks like a potato; I have to get in shape; Look at the lines on my face*) and then swap them for something else (*I'm so grateful to have this body that can give and receive love; I love myself for who I am right now; I have beautiful* [fill in the blank]). Really mean what you are saying, stick with it, and pay attention to how it feels when you treat your body with love rather than criticism.

Just remember: thought-swapping is not the same as affirmations. Personally, our experience with affirmations is that they sound good but don't really get you anywhere—likely because affirmations are something we think but rarely feel. Faking it till you make it is great and all, but you need to bring both your thoughts and feelings on board with your chosen swapped thoughts, or you'll probably just be faking it for a good long time.

If you're digging the thought-swap practice, you can take it to the next level and go on a negativity detox, where you stay alert for *any* negative self-talk and make a game of figuring out how to swap it for something better. Instead of "I have to go to work," you can think, "I *get* to go to work." Replace "I'm exhausted" with "I've had a full day and have earned a restful night's sleep." Instead of "I fucked up," try "I know how I can do better now." All of these examples replace negativity with some form of gratitude, which is one of the quickest ways to shift your feelings around something. But do keep in mind that, on average, 80 percent of our free-range thoughts are negative, so don't go so hard that you burn out.

Go for "better," not "perfect."

And go for long-term sustainable steps over fixing every single thought NOW!

SPELL-CASTING 101

The reason why a practice like thought-swapping works is because the words we use (and think) are incredibly important. Words cast spells. It's called SPELL-ING, and not by coincidence. Author Shad Helmstetter talks about this at length in his book *What to Say When You Talk to Your Self.* He writes, "The brain simply believes what you tell it most. And what you tell it about you, it will create. It has no choice."

Using words and their ultimate power for your own good is one of the quickest ways to improve your thoughts. Try not to hang out with the Big Bad Wolf in your head too often. The more you practice this, the better you'll get at noticing negative self-talk and spinning it into something a little more kind and loving. Marisa Peer, author and world-renowned hypnotist, refers to this as "speaking to your mind." You can pick exciting words that feel good to you and start to pepper your day with them. The key is to find a way to actually *feel* just a little better. Just like when swapping your thoughts, platitudes do not work here, so if you don't feel better, keep trying until you find a new thought that is authentic to you.

Beau here. I wanted to share a little phrase that I use as a personal magic spell for shifting my thoughts. It's very, very simple. I simply ask myself, "Okay! Why not?"

Believe it or not, those three little words have changed my life.

- Approach an attractive man that I'd normally never have the courage to speak to? "Okay! Why not?"
- Consider a relationship that excites me but in the past has scared me away? "Okay! Why not?"
- Dare to start a business based on my art? "Okay! Why not?"
- Write a book with my bestie about finding the freedom to love exactly the way you want? "Okay! Why not?"

Why does this work for me? Quite simply, there's something freeing about it. I'm just trying something new for the sake of trying it. I have no expectations or pressure around the outcome. It disarms my negative thought pattern completely. Instead of thinking "Why bother?", which leaves me feeling hopeless, I think "Why not?"—and it changes my energy entirely.

I encourage you to experiment with creating your own magic spell. Maybe it's "FUCK IT! Let's just try!" Or "I'm doing it anyway, because I WANT TO!" Or "Let's see what happens if . . ."

Whatever it is, tap into a sense of freedom and have fun with it. I mean, okay, why not?

A FOCUS ON FEELINGS

Ahh, feelings. The inescapable, sometimes annoying, often burdensome, and always amazing powers they wield are part of the lifelong journey of understanding ourselves. Feelings are some of the truest forms of energy. They can create tension, make you feel like you're floating, or drag you to the lowest depths of your being. And when it comes to love, feelings are always marching out and taking center stage. This is why it is so important to focus on our own feelings and how they are affecting (and sometimes exploding) our relationships.

Shannon here. When I was a teenager, I remember feeling really upset about not being liked, not having a boyfriend, not being in with the cool kids, and just feeling like an awkward outcast in general. I remember bemoaning my miserable existence to my mother, and you know what she said to me?

"Shannon, it's all in your head. You just have to decide not to feel sad."

Now, at the time I was really pissed at her for saying that.

Obviously. At that moment, my teenage self could only fume as I asked myself what she could possibly know about how hard my life was and how alone and alienated I felt. But her saying that also helped me to stop feeling so sad (mostly because I'd traded in sad for angry).

I've thought about that exchange a lot over the years. I still feel angry at her from time to time for denying my feelings of pity and self-loathing, but more often now, I see her as a saint who passed on some of the best pieces of wisdom I've ever heard. The more I think about her perspective, the more I realize that she wasn't trying to tell me not to feel my feelings—she was trying to tell me that I had it within me to make things better. She knew that the power of my thoughts could be used to transform my reaction. She was telling me that I alone had the magic within me to change my perspective and, in doing so, change my life.

I do think it's important to mention that Mom's advice comes in handy when I'm feeling a little down, but depression is a completely different beast. In this scenario I was not struggling with depression or mental health issues; I was struggling with feeling bad about myself because of high school shit. Depression and mental illness cannot be cured by positive thought alone. I've been through depression and thankfully was able to seek professional help for it.

We all have it inside ourselves to make our lives better. As we mentioned earlier, feelings and thoughts are deeply entwined, and when you learn to harness the dynamic interplay between them, you have almost unlimited power to generate new results in your life. So that's where we're turning next.

But first, we'd like to make one thing *very* clear . . .

THEY MIGHT BE IMPORTANT, BUT HONEY, FEELINGS ARE NOT FACTS

Feelings are not facts. What exactly do we mean by this?

Well, every feeling you've ever experienced—from pure joy to gut-wrenching grief—was generated by a thought in your mind. (Rarely are we even aware of the thought, but you better believe it pulled the trigger!) That thought, in turn, was generated by your internal belief system. It didn't come from a fact.

Surely, you can come up with several examples of times when your feelings and facts did not line up. Ever look in the mirror and feel repulsed by how fat you look, only to have your partner tell you how beautiful you are or your friend ask if you've been working out? Boom. Your feeling of repulsion was not based on fact. It came from a thought (*you are fat*) and an internal belief system built around the idea that fat is terrible and makes you unlovable.

Here's another classic: Have you ever felt total despair over the fact that you'll never meet anyone you'll really click with? Sweetie, there are billions of people in the world. Your despair is not based on a fact; it's based on the outlandish thought that there's absolutely no one out there for you. Dig a little deeper and you're likely to find a core belief that says you have to change to be loved. Look to your past and you may see a pattern of getting into relationships with people you feel are "beneath you," or, worse yet, getting into relationships where you allow yourself to be treated like shit.

Are you starting to see how this is all connected?

Welcome to the matrix, baby.

LET IT GO

Feelings are entwined with thoughts; you can't have one without the other.

Earlier, we learned that we can embrace a practice that targets our thoughts in order to change our feelings. Guess what? It goes both ways! Yes, girl, you *can* put your thing down, flip it, and reverse it! So if you're someone who would rather practice working with your feelings in order to shift negative thoughts and toxic beliefs, we've got you.

One of the quickest ways to disrupt negative feelings is to let them out and let them go.

Feelings may not be facts, but that doesn't mean they aren't important, and they shouldn't be invalidated or ignored. Far from it. It's important to acknowledge your feelings and experience your tough experiences. If you truly do that, you will be able to let them go.

Kids are masters at this. They are not defined by their feelings; they just experience them. Take tantrums, for example. A kid can have a massive freak-out about something (often over something you as an adult don't even understand), and then, ten minutes later, be smiling, chatting, and acting like whatever shit they were losing their mind about wasn't even a thing.

As adults, we don't allow ourselves this luxury. Most of us were taught from an early age not to cry, that emotions are a sign of weakness, and all that other toxic shit. Admittedly, it would be pretty weird to see an adult having a tantrum on the sidewalk, but in the comfort of your own home, we say go for it if you need to release those big feelings. Get that energy and those feelings out of your body. Wave bye-bye as you release them out into the world. Not only does this exercise feel good, but it will also allow you to bring a sense of clarity and perspective to your situation that you may not have been able to experience if you were caught up in all of your feels. Feeling your feelings and then releasing them allows you to step outside of yourself and see the situation for what it really is.

What you don't want to do, however, is go home and dump your feelings on your significant others. This is the opposite of what we are talking about. When we talk about not invalidating your feelings, we mean that you need to validate yourself. The moment you expect your validation to come from someone else, you are kissing your power good-bye. We are talking about being responsible for your feelings, not participating in drama and codependency (more on that in chapter 9).

REPLACE *FEELING* WITH *BEING*

So, what about those moments when we can't run home and have an emotional meltdown? As adults, we are often in professional and personal spaces where we are required to keep our shit together. Even if feelings are arising, no one is offering us a tantrum tea break. For cases such as this, we've come up with a little exercise where we replace *feeling* with *being*.

We do this by noticing (yes, that ol' chestnut again) when feelings are showing up, and then disrupting them by asking a question in that moment: "How am I being?"

This deceptively simple practice can be a pattern-disrupting and eye-opening experience.

> **Beau here.** I'd like to share a personal example of utilizing this practice. I'm an introvert by nature, but I have a front-facing job and a life where interactions with people are necessary. I often catch myself on set, at social events, or even just at a party, hanging back and watching instead of participating. In these moments I'm usually feeling overwhelmed, insecure, and

worried. But I've learned to notice when these feelings arise and to pause to ask myself, "How am I *being* at this moment?"

This question helps me to shift perspective from a focus on my private interior world to a consideration of my impact on the outer world: If someone were observing me, what would they see? How am I being? When I can take a step away from my feelings, I can see that I'm being reserved, unapproachable, and quiet.

I've spent years in self-inquiry, so I now know that this deep avoidance when I'm with others stems from a childhood of being bullied and a core belief that if I let people see me, they will hurt me. And it's good to know that, but truthfully, at that party, it doesn't really matter. I don't need to know *why* I am feeling a certain way; I only need to know what I am going to do about it (because this practice is all about moving from the interior world to the exterior world!).

So, once I have established how I am being or how I might be perceived by an outside observer, I can ask myself, "How would I *like* to be?" Outgoing? Friendly? Inquisitive? Kind? Whatever the answer, I decide to simply try. And every time, it turns out well. Every. Single. Time.

In much the same way as with my "Okay, why not?" practice, I find it easier if I treat this process like a game. I say to myself, "I wonder what would happen if I shifted my way of being?" And suddenly, like magic, it's as if the entire day's energy changes. Someone on the crew or in the room says something that res- onates with me, or suggests a great book, or a contact, or brings me another job. Just the other day, I ended up meet- ing an attractive guy and making a connection. The important thing, though, is that I don't do this to *get* anything. I let go of any expectations and just do it to live a better life. I think that energy comes across as authentic, which helps people feel comfortable. By playing it like it's a game, it actually doesn't really matter if people respond well or not. There are no stakes beyond having a better day and possibly learning something new, and it really does get easier every time.

BETTER TOGETHER—THE MIND/BODY CONNECTION

Okay, class, quick review.

We've looked at ways to hack your thoughts, and we've explored methods for disrupting feelings. You know what's next, right? Of course you do.

We're going to look at how to work with your thoughts and feelings in tandem. When you can harness their twin powers, you'll reach your destination doubly fast.

The reason for this is pretty simple. Thoughts are the domain of the mind. Feelings are the domain of the body. When you think about something embarrassing, your cheeks will flush in response. When confronted with a conflict situation, your heart may start to race. When thinking about a new love interest, your tummy fills with butterflies.

Dr. Bruce Lipton addresses this body/mind connection. According to his findings, our very genes are changed by the environment we are in, and there are a number of physical illnesses that are triggered by internal stressors and toxic thoughts. Our body responds to our mind. He writes, "What we believe, we become." We couldn't agree more, which is why any practice geared toward shedding old toxic beliefs in order to choose new ones is always going to be more effective when the whole team is on board.

REACH FOR THE NEXT BEST FEELING THOUGHT

When we talked about swapping thoughts, we looked at the power of taking a negative thought and swapping it for a positive one. But, real talk—sometimes that's not always possible. Life isn't a bubble-gum fantasy, and sometimes shit gets dark and hard. There will definitely be moments when you can't rally to come up with a positive thought that feels even remotely true. That doesn't mean you're a failure; it means you're in a hard place. This is when it helps to recruit your feelings to assist.

One of the easiest ways to do this involves the Abraham-Hicks Emotional Guidance Scale and the concept of reaching for the next best *feeling thought*.

In their book *Ask and It Is Given*, Esther Hicks and Jerry Hicks identify the twenty-two most commonly felt emotions. As seen below, they are arranged on a scale from highest vibration (most positive) to lowest vibration (most negative).

The Abraham-Hicks Emotional Guidance Scale

1. Joy/Appreciation/Empowerment/Freedom/Love
2. Passion
3. Enthusiasm/Eagerness/Happiness
4. Positive Expectation/Belief
5. Optimism
6. Hopefulness
7. Contentment
8. Boredom
9. Pessimism
10. Frustration/Irritation/Impatience
11. Overwhelment (feeling overwhelmed)
12. Disappointment
13. Doubt
14. Worry
15. Blame
16. Discouragement
17. Anger
18. Revenge
19. Hatred/Rage
20. Jealousy
21. Insecurity/Guilt/Unworthiness
22. Fear/Grief/Desperation/Despair/Powerlessness

The concept of reaching for the next best feeling thought is pretty straightforward. Rather than attempting to move from anger to optimism (a large jump on the scale), maybe just reach for the next thought that has a *slightly* better feeling. If, for example, you can come up with a thought that moves you from feeling angry to feeling discouraged, or possibly to feeling blame, it is still a step in the right direction (like when teenaged Shannon moved from despair to anger). Basically, any move upward is a good move, and eventually you will have the energy to reach for the *next* best feeling thought. You have a lifetime to practice this, and there is no getting it perfect. Better, yes. Perfect, no.

FACE YOUR FEARS, TAKE ACTION

In our experience, one of the most difficult feelings to disrupt is fear. That's because fear is primal and isn't easily swayed by thoughts or intentions. When dealing with fear, the trick is to also bring action into the thought/feeling mix in order to recondition your fear response. We're sure you've heard this famous quote: "The definition of insanity is doing the same thing over and over and expecting different results." But when it comes to gathering new evidence to evict your fear, this is exactly what you'll be doing.

> **Shannon again.** I'm an incredibly conflict-averse person. Someone so much as gives me a side-eye glance when they change lanes next to me and my heart rate goes up a notch. I avoid arguments and disagreements at all costs—historically at the cost of my own boundaries and eventually my relationships—because the thought of being in conflict with someone makes my hands shake, and my thoughts become a tangled ball of string.

Not many people enjoy conflict, so I know I'm not alone here. But still, I wanted to be better at confronting difficult situations, so I sought out a practice that would help me accomplish this.

I knew that my beliefs concerning conflict were deeply buried, so I started with the intention to replace my belief that I am terrible at conflict with the belief that I am strong in conflict and good at it. Next, I chose some positive thoughts: *I am able to manage conflict with a clear mind and calm body. I can negotiate for the results I desire.*

Then came the hard part. I knew I couldn't just think or feel my way out of this. I needed to take deliberate action to put myself in situations that would allow me to work through the emotional/feeling-based reactions in my body: racing heart, tense muscles, flushed and clammy skin. I initiated conversations where I knew the other person might not feel comfortable with what I needed to communicate, such as providing tough feedback with my employees at work or having that difficult conversation with my ex-husband about our children. I wasn't always great at it, but I did it over and over again until I created a new level of comfort with conflict and shifted that outdated belief out the door. (Full disclosure: The belief still moves back in from time to time. I think I need to ask for my key back.)

I didn't learn how to do this all on my own. I have a friend who is a master at managing conflict. He owns some super-fancy-pants restaurants, and he can walk into any meeting and say the shit that everyone else is too afraid to say and feel completely and utterly comfortable doing it. I've always been inspired by his confidence, so I asked him for some guidance. Turns out, it didn't come naturally for him either. He confessed that he used to be terrified of conflict, and that not all altercations turned out well. He just kept telling himself he could do it and kept practicing until he had enough results under his belt to prove it. Now he's able to have really difficult, courageous conversations and stay cool as a cucumber.

Now that's something I can aspire to.

YOUR VIBRATION IS A MAGNET

This is a book with a focus on romantic relationships. That doesn't mean the other people in your life are secondary in importance. That couldn't be further from the truth. (Girl, don't lose touch with your friends every time you're into a new guy!)

There is nothing quite like a supportive community of like-minded people to help you on your road to growth. These are your friends, teachers, guides, mentors—all of the people who make up your larger network of support—and it's equally important to invest in building and nurturing these relationships.

If you don't feel you have these types of people in your life, all it takes to find them is a shift of focus. The law of vibration states that everything in the universe moves. Nothing is immune. Everything is energy. Like attracts like. In many ways, the universe is the ultimate magic mirror. To quote Esther Hicks and Jerry Hicks once more: "The Universe responds to your vibrational offering, to your point of attraction, to the thoughts you think, and to the way you feel."

The universe reflects back to you that which you choose to see.

We've talked about this when it comes to your love life. If you see yourself as someone who doesn't deserve an abundance of love, or someone who thinks those things are just out of reach, these become your beliefs, and, ultimately, all of your actions will bring this belief to pass.

If you think all men are frogs, get ready for a plague of 'em.

This law holds true when it comes to attracting the people in your life. Self-help author and Law of Attraction expert Bob Proctor commonly teaches the concept that you can only attract *to* you what is in harmonious vibration *with* you. In other words, your vibration is a magnet.

THE ALCHEMIST'S FORMULA: BE. DO. HAVE.

We would like to share one last practice that combines all the elements of thoughts, feelings, and actions and brings them into alignment with the Law of Attraction theory. We call it the Alchemist's Formula.

When it comes to personal growth or obtaining our goals, many of us are very busy *doing* something so that we can *have* something in order to *be* something. We call this misguided pursuit the Do, Have, Be Formula.

We know—it's a bit confusing, so here's an example: "If I work out and eat right (Do), then I will have a great body (Have), and I will be attractive (Be)."

More often than not, the ultimate goal of what we are trying to *be* is holding a deeper secret about how we view ourselves, and it is therefore well worth exploring. One way to do this is by asking yourself a question: "How will I *feel* when I get the thing I want?" This question allows you to move beyond the superficial goal to get at the deeper desires beneath it. Perhaps if you are attractive, then you will *feel* like you are enough? Or you may finally *feel* like you are lovable or desirable.

Maybe your goals are focused on *doing* what is needed to *have* financial security so you can *be* successful. Why? How will you *feel* once you have the money you seek? Perhaps if you get that big house you'll *feel* safe in a world that has always felt frightening to you. Perhaps you will finally *feel* like you've earned the right to be choosy in love because you bring something of value to the relationship.

When you take a moment to drill down into the motivations driving the Do, Have, Be Formula, you will usually find that you are running a program of striving. And the goals you've set are simply setting you up to feel like you have never truly arrived.

Let's be clear here: there is absolutely nothing wrong with wanting things or having goals. On the contrary, we encourage getting everything you've ever wanted, which is why we'd like to introduce the Alchemist's Formula. Instead of Do, Have, Be, we've changed it to Be, Do, Have.

An example: Imagine being in a relationship with a great partner.

How would you *be* in that relationship?

Maybe you'd be spontaneous, loving, creative, and caring.

Building on the concept that like attracts like, it follows that you need to start *being* those things right now.

How? Start *doing* things that are spontaneous, creative, and caring in order to attract that great partner. Don't wait to be in the relationship. Start now.

You can make a deliberate decision today to *be* more spontaneous and start *doing* more fun and exciting things. Or you could decide to *be* more loving and start *doing* things to show your love for the people in your life.

By making that conscious choice, you have leveled up your vibrations and you will start to attract the things you are giving off. The likelihood of meeting a partner who shares these qualities and *having* that relationship is now much higher. And because you are running a program of creating abundance (rather than striving to attain something to fill your lack), you are having an amazing time and a really great life with the people around you right now.

Best of all, there is no arriving—because you are already here.

Which is great news, because a life of personal growth is not about the final destination; it really is about the road you are taking.

And, baby, you have an exciting road ahead of you!

Unlike Cinderella, you aren't a passenger in the back of the pumpkin carriage. You've got the tools now to grab the reins and steer yourself out of the land of fairy tales and into your own magical kingdom.

So let's get going.

CHAPTER 5

PUT IT TOGETHER AND WHAT HAVE YOU GOT: BIBBIDI-BOBBIDI-CHOOSE

Quick, what's your favorite coffee order from your favorite café?

Is it an Americano with an extra shot of espresso, room for cream? Macchiato extra hot? Mochaccino extra foam? Regular drip, black? Double-double (for all you Canadians out there)?

Oh wait. We haven't even considered the fact that maybe you prefer tea. You might be the type of person who tries something new every time, or you might be someone who loves waking up and knowing you are going to have the exact same drink every day for the rest of your life. We'll likely never guess, because these days there are about as many ways to take your morning beverage as there are individuals on this planet. That's because we live in the age of choice.

For a recent article in the *Guardian*, headlined "Where Belief Is Born," Alok Jha spoke to neuroscientist Kathleen Taylor. "In the West, most of our physical needs are provided for," Taylor said. "We have a level of luxury and civilization that is pretty much unparalleled. That leaves us with a lot more leisure and more space in our heads for thinking." Taylor also stated that beliefs and ideas have become our currency, and pointed out that society is no longer about survival but about choice—choice of companion, political views, options, and ideas.

We are living in an age abundant with choice. Customization is the new normal. So why, then, are we all expected to order up the exact same type of relationship? Why should everyone want the same thing?

Imagine a world where you could custom design your relationship in the same way you would a cup of coffee. If everything was on the table for consideration—monogamy, gender, sex, how much time you'd spend together, what you'd do together, the reason you are together, the ideal duration of your relationship, if you live together or not—do you know what you would order? We'd love for you to be able to rattle that off as quickly as your drink order at Starbucks, because we think that it's *slightly* more important. And for the record, you don't have to imagine the world we just described. It's real. It's here. You *can* choose the exact relationship you want.

If the shoe don't fit, honey, smash it.

Start being responsible for your life. And yes, we mean *being* responsible, not taking responsibility. It's another subtle spell. *Taking* responsibility assumes that responsibility is something that exists outside of ourselves, but *being* responsible is a deliberate choice, a way of being. Recognizing that we are generating our reality with our beliefs, thoughts, and feelings, and understanding that we have the power to change and to choose, is what being responsible is all about. Why so choosy? Because every time you make a choice, you are stepping into your power and standing in the center of your own life.

CHOOSE VERSUS CHOSEN

I can promise you that any time you are desperate to be chosen, it's a deep calling to choose yourself. —TORY ELETTO

If only Cinderella had been following New York–based therapist Tory Eletto on Instagram. This little nugget right here might have saved her from her desperate desire to be chosen. Why is it that so many of us want to be chosen and are so reluctant to choose for ourselves? It is as if being chosen is supposed to prove something about you. But all it really "proves" is that you are willing to hand over your self-worth and value to another person—sometimes a virtual stranger—rather than to yourself.

Choosing ourselves is so hard precisely because it's not based on someone else. It's rooted in the idea that it all rests on you. You hold all the power, and at the end of the day, it's up to you to create the life, and the relationships, you want.

When we sat down with Lisa Kalmin, author of *The Problem Is How You See the Problem*, she explained that choosing to choose (which we define as choosing not from your past beliefs but based on your actual wants, needs, and desires in the moment, without expectation of outcome) "is not based on a condition, or someone else, or on your circumstances, or some history, or something you thought you were supposed to do or be. Choosing comes from a place of possibility. It creates a blank canvas."

Blank canvases and blank pages can be scary. Have you ever looked at a blank piece of paper and thought, *Where do I start?*

Well, you pick up any one of the tools we've provided and you just start playing. Add some words to that page through the power of your choices. Start now. Sure, you might make some mistakes along the way, but it's in the imperfections and the discomfort where the learnings and the beauty are. So go ahead and fill up the whole page. Don't worry about staying in the lines, and be sure to fill up all the corners and edges as you write the story of your big beautiful life.

A funny thing will start to happen when you begin to reprogram yourself about that desire to be chosen. The minute you start to choose yourself, to take action to change those beliefs, thoughts, and feelings that are no longer serving you, you'll start vibrating at a new frequency. You'll begin to attract more of what you want. You'll start to meet different people. You may even find yourself ready to go for a new relationship. And when you do, you'll know that you're choosing it, not waiting around like a passive Cinderwench for life and love to happen to you.

Listen.

You are a treasure.

A straight-up gem.

Don't cheapen your life by waiting for someone else to prove that to you. And whatever you do, don't press the pause button on your life while you wait for someone else to choose you. Raise the bar. Kiss your life. This might mean travel, moving, or starting a family—all of this is possible without a romantic relationship. Because, ultimately, what we've been talking about isn't how to be a better person, or how to change your relationships with other people, or even how to get into a romantic relationship. It's about changing your relationship with yourself, first and foremost.

You now have everything you need. You've flowed through the process of identifying your hidden limiting beliefs, breaking old patterns, and harnessing the power of your thoughts and feelings in order to pro-actively choose the life you want. You possess the power to choose who you want to be and who you want to be with, and you now have the keys to whatever kingdom you would like to explore.

Understand this: Choice is freedom. Freedom is power.

Sans fairy godmother.

PART TWO

Happily Ever After . . .

CHAPTER 6

YOU CAN BE YOUR HERO, BABY

H APPILY EVER AFTER . . . that's how all our newly wed (and newly met) fairy-tale couples lived out their days—immediately after they legally sealed their union according to the dictates of state and church. But what happens next? What does happily ever after even look like? We'll never know. Apparently, the authors didn't feel this part of the story was necessary for their target audience of young readers. According to fairy tales, a relationship is a fixed destination point that you reach, thus signaling the end of your journey.

Moral: You've been chosen. You will live out the rest of your days in gratitude for this singular act. Your desires have now been met, and you'd better not have any others. The End.

That's *so* like a fairy tale. They promise a goose that lays golden eggs, but all you end up with is an oversized barnyard bird that shits all over your house.

So, this is where we are going to begin—at the end of the fairy tale, a.k.a. the beginning of a relationship.

WUV, SWEET WUV

So, you've met someone whom you really like. We're talking butterflies, sweaty palms, and nervous laughter. That melting feeling you get when you kiss. The way time shifts to lightspeed and hours feel like minutes. It's all rather intoxicating, and we hope you enjoy the moment to its fullest. This feeling doesn't come around every day, and if you've been doing your work to identify and choose the relationship that's right for you, then you're really tapping into a magical time filled with sunshine, rainbows, and dancing unicorns. Drink deeply of that elixir of new love, my friend. But do remember that this feeling you are having—while clearly a wonderful part of a relationship—is not the whole point.

When some cloud cover rolls in and blocks out your sunshine and the unicorns foxtrot off and take their rainbows with them, it does not mean your relationship is doomed. You don't need to spend all of your energy trying to recapture that first flush of love. That's not the point either.

Love isn't a destination, or a possession, or something that needs to be perfect all the time. But it is something that can be mastered. According to Miguel Ruiz, author of *The Mastery of Love*, "To become masters of love we have to practice love. The art of relationship is also a whole mastery, and the only way to reach mastery is with practice."

This is why we spent the first half of this book focusing on how to practice these principles and apply them to our own lives *first*—so you could be the best possible you for you, and then bring that version of yourself into the relationship of your choosing. It's not about being loved no matter what; it's an act of attention toward yourself and another in order to practice and grow. That's the point!

RELATIONSHIPS TAKE GROWTH

Have you ever been told that relationships take work? Yeah, so have we. Who came up with this genius concept? And why do we all accept it as a fact of life?

Let's pretend for a minute that you've just signed up to join a country club. We haven't been to a country club, but we imagine them to be pristine places where the grass is as green as emeralds; the lobster buffet is always piled high; and the pool is attended to by gorgeous, shirtless pool boys who bring us cool towels all day long. Now what if, just before signing up for this membership, you were told that belonging to this country club would be a lot of work. Wouldn't you pause before signing that piece of paper and say "Huh"? Maybe it depends on how cute those pool boys are, but we're betting that no one with any sense would want to sign up for something that takes work when it's supposed to be enjoyable—especially if they're expected to pay for it! Yet we all happily agree that relationships take work and we are 100 percent okay with that. We sign on the dotted line and accept that we're gonna have to work our asses off for the rest of our lives. Well, we call bullshit on that. Because relationships don't take work. Relationships take growth.

You didn't think all the growth stuff was going to be over after part one, did you? Not a chance. In fact, this is where things really start to get interesting. There's personal growth and then there's *relational* growth. That means if you want to learn how to be an awesome partner in a relationship, you need to practice this *in* a relationship. Be warned: you may experience a resurgence of Cinderella Syndrome the moment you get into a relationship, no matter how studiously you prepared. Relax, you are not relapsing. This is normal. It just means that you have a few more fairy-tale beliefs hidden away somewhere. Luckily, your relationship will help you to identify them, if you are open to the process.

Finally, there are certain core beliefs that come from early relational wounds. If you picked up the belief in childhood that you are fundamentally unlovable, this is not something that you can heal entirely on your own. Relational wounds are healed relationally. You unlearn such a belief through the conscious practice of giving and receiving love.

Imago relationship therapy was developed by Dr. Harville Hendrix and Dr. Helen LaKelly Hunt in 1980. *Imago* is the Latin word for "image" and refers to the "unconscious image of familiar love." Hendrix and Hunt's research uncovered the frequent connection between difficult childhood experiences and issues manifesting in adult relationships. Our brains crave the familiar, and as adults we unconsciously seek out the comfort of the known. We are often attracted to people who are similar to our caregivers, even if the traits they possess are not healthy ones for us. Many of us end up in relationships with someone who (often even physically) resembles a parent. We *know*—horrifying but true. But this is why whatever issues we had in our familial relationships are likely to come up over and over again in our romantic relationships.

Let's use our darling Cinderella as an example. Applying Imago theory, we could argue that Cinderella had a foundational need to be chosen and loved by Prince Charming because her father abandoned her (no shade, he just dies—at least in the animated Disney version). She believed that she would only be safe and happy with a man who loved her so much he was willing to scour the countryside to find her perfectly dainty little foot. And you can bet that the first time the prince's royal duties require him to travel to some other county, Cinderella isn't going to be happy about it. Instead of enjoying some me-time, she's gonna complain about how many nights he'll be away. She's gonna ask him if she can tag along so she won't be alone. She may even go so far as to give Charming the silent treatment. Too bad Cinderella never learned that we all have childhood wounds that will sometimes rear their irrational little heads in our relationships, and that this is the opportunity to finally heal those old wounds and be free of them once and for all.

LOVE IS UNDERSTANDING

It's so easy to assume that, having spent tons of time and effort building yourself into a strong, confident, and competent individual, this is something you'll maintain effortlessly once in a relationship. Truthfully, relationships will trigger your shit in ways you might never have anticipated. Not only are you going to have to deal with *your* shit, but you're also going to have to deal with someone else's—which often you won't understand because your lens on life is totally different from theirs. After all, every relationship is composed of two different but intertwined realities. Sounds scary, right? It is! But it's also sort of exciting. The person standing before you isn't just asking you to love them, they are asking you to understand them.

Because that's what love is—understanding.

Understanding another and understanding yourself.

That's why we just can't wrap our heads around the Cindy story. How can she and Princey fall in love without knowing a single thing about each other, except that they both like to get dressed up and dance all night? Admittedly, we've met a few people this way, but we never actually wanted to ride off into the sunset with any of them. If anything, we found ourselves doing the walk of shame the next day.

A word of caution, lovelies: If you're with someone who isn't willing to grow with you, or at least try to understand the growth you're going through, you might want to ask yourself if this is the relationship for you. You might want to think about your frequency. Two people who aren't committed to growing together eventually start to vibrate on different frequencies. And that? That can create a whole lot of static. But when two people are committed to showing up as their best selves in a relationship and ready to focus their intentional curiosity on truly understanding their chosen partner, the transformative energy that can be generated is nothing short of magical. *This* is what being in a conscious relationship is all about.

THE CONSCIOUS RELATIONSHIP

Let's break it down.

You cannot be in a solid, loving, and supportive relationship without owning your shit. If you really want to start seeing a shift from fantasy to real connection, you need to start being responsible for what you're carrying around with you in relation to someone else. Let's say you struggle a bit with insecurity. You tell yourself that you protect yourself because you have to. People tell you that you are defensive, and sure, you know you struggle with this. But that's because any suggestions about acting differently or changing feel like criticism to you, but *that's* because you grew up feeling like you have to be perfect and besides—

We're sorry to interrupt, but have you noticed what's happening here?

This is where self-awareness sometimes trips us up. We can get really good at justifying our own behavior because we know what is going on internally. But no one else does. On the outside, we just come off as a defensive jerk. We have to go beyond understanding what's going on inside our own heads; we have to own our impact on the outside world too. Because when we get defensive, that's us projecting our shit onto someone else, and that's poisonous to relationships. What if, instead, you took all of those internal processing skills that allow you to love and accept even your less-than-lovely bits and channeled them into your relationship? When your partner does something that you don't like or understand, you now have the skills to get curious about what their deeper motivations/reasons/protections may be.

Two people in a conscious relationship are able to bravely take a look at their past and identify why their feelings of abandonment, jealousy, resentment, or rejection are cropping up. They are able to understand that these feelings are not a result of the relationship but of the self that is participating within the relationship. They know who they are, and they want to know the entirety of who their partner is too.

Conscious relationships put growth first and foremost. As Brian Andreas—author, artist, and publisher—wrote, "It changes how you decide to live when you decide to love each other without knowing how it ends."

The couple in a conscious relationship understands that growth, not eternity, is the goal. That's not to say they don't worry about the relationship ending, or that they don't talk about where the relationship is going, or that they don't fantasize about having some sparkly wedding. All of that can happen. But growth always comes first. Growth is always the happily ever after.

BE YOUR OWN HERO

One of the key concepts we are going to explore in the second part of this book is the idea of choosing to "be your own hero." In essence, you are continuing to apply the Alchemist's Formula *in* a relationship, *for* your relationship.

This means that you need to be the person you want to be in a relationship with. If you want to be with a strong, sensitive partner, you get to be that. You show up as a champion in order to receive a champion in return. If you want a best friend who has your back no matter what, well . . . you know the drill.

Being your own hero means you aren't waiting passively for someone else to make the first move. You are large and in charge—in charge of your vulnerability, your willingness to accept love, and your capacity to truly listen and show up for someone. Most important, you are in charge of your commitment to authenticity.

Brené Brown, professor, author, lecturer and podcast host, said it best: "Authenticity is the daily practice of letting go of who we think we're supposed to be and embracing who we are."

Ain't nothing more heroic than being your true, authentic self and then sharing that self with someone else.

At the end of part one, we asked you to imagine what kind of relationship you'd like to be in. As we begin part two, we'd like you to envision how this relationship actually works and how you and your partner relate to one another. Imagine a relationship where there is room for both of you to figure out why certain things trigger you the way they do. Where expectations and drama are checked at the door, and bravery and vulnerability around communication is standard practice. Where you both feel seen, heard, and understood because you've stepped away from your own defenses and have taken the time to be open and curious about each other. Where the problems that come up between you are embraced as opportunities to invent solutions that respect both of your individual needs.

Sounds nice, doesn't it?

Welcome to love outside the fairy tale. We think you'll like it here.

As your own hero, you wield the Sword of Inquiry, which can slice through the enchanted vines that threaten to choke the new growth in your relationships and slash through the briars that deny you your freedom. In the following chapters we will examine the most common (and noxious) threats to all of you brave souls looking to enter or currently in a relationship.

Jump on your steed. Let's ride.

CHAPTER 7

WHAT TO EXPECT WHEN YOU'RE EXPECTING (CERTAIN THINGS FROM YOUR RELATIONSHIP)

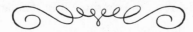

SHAKESPEARE, AUTHOR OF THE romantic tragedy *Romeo and Juliet*, has been credited with saying, "Expectation is the root of all heartache." Turns out he never really said that, but as the man responsible for the most fucked-up relationship story ever, he oughta know.

Unfortunately, expectations within a relationship are almost impossible to avoid. Expectations are sort of like beliefs, but the type of expectations we're talking about are the kind that involve other people. Also similar to your beliefs, most expectations are buried deep in the subconscious mind, like an active land mine, just waiting for the right person to come along and put their foot in juuuuuuust the wrong place.

KABLOOIE!

Hey, Shakespeare: expectations are also the root of many a breakup.

The root of the word *expectation* comes from the Latin word *expectationem*, which translates to "an awaiting." So, what are you waiting for? To be disappointed? Disappointment is a part of all relationships. At some point your partner is not going to meet your expectations, and you won't meet theirs either. It's up to both of you to choose what to do about it. It doesn't have to be an explosive event, but if you want to avoid an expectation detonation, you're going to have to go after those buried expectations in much the same way you went after your buried beliefs—you'll need to locate them, dig them up, and identify them. But unlike with beliefs, this isn't solitary work. Once you've identified your expectations, you will be sharing them in order to modify them, or possibly toss them out completely. You can pop some nice standards and boundaries into the hole left behind, and you're all set.

That, dear readers, is Expectation Diffusion 101, and that's what we're going to cover in this chapter. So grab your shovel and let's get hunting.

DON'T SHOULD ALL OVER YOURSELF

How do you spot expectations? It's simple. Expectations are often cloaked in "shoulds." He *should* have saved Friday night for us, not gone out with his friends. She *should* appreciate me more. He *shouldn't* bring his phone to bed. You might want to take a moment and ask yourself: Are you shoulding all over your relationships?

Seriously, you don't want to waste time and energy on what someone *should* be doing. But *should* can be an incredibly useful word, because when you notice yourself using it, you have the opportunity to get really clear on the expectation that is underneath it. You can use that *should* to better understand your expectations and also to communicate to your partner what you *really* want and why.

To flush your wants from the shadows and put yourself on the fast track to understanding what's driving your expectations, you simply need to put the *should* statement to the side and ask yourself instead: "What do I *want* from my partner?"

This reframing is subtle but powerful. A *should* indicates that there is some universal law in place. Let's face it, these expectations disguised as *shoulds* are so common, almost everyone thinks they are true. "We should spend the weekend together because we're in a relationship." But reframing to "I want us to spend the weekend together" reminds you that this is personal. Or, returning to the example above, if you want him to spend Friday with you and not his friends, that's fine, but understand that this comes from your wants, not his. And he, in turn, may want very different things. (Hello, welcome to a relationship!)

Once you've identified what you want, the next step is to ask yourself *why* you want it. Why, for example, do you want Friday nights with your romantic partner? You may want to know that he still loves being with you, or you may want reassurance that she isn't taking you for granted, or you may want to do things with his friends too and not feel excluded . . . the list goes on. Unless you can understand and identify your wants, you'll never crack your expectations and how they might be damaging your relationship. And you'll certainly never be able to fully communicate your wants in a productive way.

Once you understand that your expectation around your boyfriend keeping every Friday as a date night comes from wanting assurance that he still loves spending time with you, then you can have a very different conversation. You don't have to get sucked into an exhausting dialogue about him abandoning you to spend time with his friends, one in which you explain, he defends, and both of you go round and round the issue while missing the point entirely. Rather, you can simply state that it's important for you to know that he wants to spend time with you and that you are a priority. Same want, two totally different ways of communicating your needs. This also allows space for your significant other to suggest alternative ways to address what you want, aside from the one action that you thought he *should* do.

Human connection specialist Mark Groves addressed this very thing when we met with him to discuss tactics for communicating expectations. Groves reminded us that it's in the hearing of our own voice that we can change a pattern. Simply by communicating expectations we're already in a place where we can break our old relational patterns. (Yup, expectations also create patterns. We *told* you they were a lot like beliefs!)

According to Groves, "Expectations are more correlated to 'nice-to-haves.'" He went on to explain that it's all in the way we express and frame them. "Hearing 'when I'm upset, I expect you to bring me flowers,' . . . if someone said that to me I'd be like, 'Fuck that!'" he told us. "But if I learned what your love language is by you saying, 'It's really nice when I'm upset for you to do nice things for me,' that's different. It also allows the other person to participate in the *act* rather than having to be a certain way."

Keep in mind that your partner may not have anticipated your want, so you may wish to offer some space for alignment. You should also allow space for someone to challenge your wants. You did all this great thinking ahead of time, but your partner is just hearing it now. Go gently. And remember, just because you want something doesn't make it right.

Finally, it's great to keep in mind that your partner may have some *shoulds* of their own that are impossible for you to anticipate but seem pretty unreasonable on the surface of things.

These conversations can be intimidating at first. As Groves reminds us, "It's the fear of disappointment that leads us to not have the conversation [because] of the fear of rejection. But the actual having of the conversation is the victory."

If you can learn to create a practice of gentle inquiry into the *shoulds* both you and your partner are bringing to the relationship, then you have every chance to defuse those puppies before they blow.

THE HAPPINESS DISCONNECT

Setting your radar for *should* phrases will help you detect expectations that are not being met and those you need to explore. But what about those that *are* being met but still aren't making you happy? To locate these expectations, we like to focus our attention on the Happiness Disconnect.

What's that?

Songstress Sheryl Crow may have explained it best when she crafted an entire song around the idea that what makes you happy shouldn't make you sad. This perfectly captures the concept of the Happiness Disconnect—which is when the anticipated happiness around attaining/achieving something doesn't line up with your actual happiness.

Another way to put it: you get what you think you want and you're still not happy.

This, my friend, is a big, waving red flag that is planted squarely on an unrealistic expectation.

We have a friend we'll call High-Expectations Heather. She's confident, successful, and knows exactly how she should be treated in a relationship—like a million bucks. She's got her shit figured out. Her expectations are very clear from the moment of the first date. The man must book the date, text the next day, and be able to hold a good conversation and the door. His style must speak of money but not arrogant flash. There are many, many rules. And that's before she even gets into a relationship. She calls it "weeding out the frogs."

She's been single for a long time even though that is not what she wants.

Just when we were starting to wonder if Heather's expectations were going to prevent any man from soaring over that sky-high bar (we believe in raising the bar, but maybe not to the stratosphere), she met someone. He was perfect! He did all the things and ticked all the boxes, and their relationship moved very quickly. Before long, Heather had moved into the penthouse that he owned (also on her list). A few weeks later we were out having drinks with Heather; we congratulated her on holding out for what she knew she wanted. Happiness at last for Heather!

"He's perfect," she agreed, and then burst into tears as she took a sip of chardonnay. "He's everything I thought I wanted, but I'm just not feeling it. What's wrong with me?"

Heather was experiencing a big fat case of the Happiness Disconnect. What she thought she wanted and what she actually needed were at odds, but she didn't realize this *until she got what she wanted*. Turns out her impossibly high expectations were actually a protection mechanism. She wasn't "weeding out the frogs" after all. She was just scared shitless to have her heart broken, so she built walls disguised as expectations to keep the kingdom of her heart protected. Placing expectations on every man she met was her way of ensuring that she never put herself in a position of vulnerability ever again. And when a man finally climbed over all those walls to meet her? He just wasn't the one. She thought fulfilling her expectations would make her happy, but it didn't. And that, friends, is a Happiness Disconnect.

Expectations are not always what they appear to be. If you are experiencing a Happiness Disconnect in your life, pay attention. You likely have some expectations that are acting like a mirage and leading you in the wrong direction. But it is possible there is something else at play as well. Sometimes our Happiness Disconnect is due to the fact that we are dealing with an addiction to disappointment.

Mark Groves broke this one down for us. "People who learn to use expectation in a way to manipulate and control and hold something over someone's head all the time, they're addicted to disappointment," he says. "And I see this in relationships, especially when one person in the relationship says, 'I feel like nothing I ever do is right.' Truthfully, that person *can't* do anything right, because the goal is to never let them. Because if I let you start doing things right, then I might have to soften and surrender and let you in."

Whoa, did you just spot some walls around your kingdom? Are you using expectations to protect yourself in a relationship? Have you ever thought about what might happen if you could accept disappointment? Because sometimes allowing for a little disappointment can lead to a much deeper, richer, and more truthful place for both of you.

EXPECTATIONS VS. STANDARDS

Up to this point, we've largely been exploring how to identify, talk about, and maybe even eliminate unrealistic or unnecessary expectations from your life. But we want to take a moment to make an important distinction between expectations and standards.

Standards are a good thing. In fact, they're necessary. It can some-times be tricky to tell the difference between standards and expectations, though, especially when they are your own.

Think of it this way: expectations are negotiable, and standards are what we like to think of as immovable objects.

Standards stem from our values, and they are the nonnegotiable things that you need to have in a partner. Standards differ for all of us, but they might be things like needing a certain level of affection; respect for your time, needs, and ambitions; a commitment to spending time together; interest in your hobbies, history, and what makes you tick; inti-macy (and not just physical); affection for your family; and generosity.

Expectations are something else entirely. They are primarily what we've been addressing here because they are the cause of most relation-ship woes. An example of an expectation is the assumption that your partner should know what you want or need just because they love you. Are you dating the Long Island Medium? That type of expectation is completely unfair. Another common expectation is that just because you and your partner love each other, you should like all the same things and agree on all the same issues. That may sound lovely in theory, but it would get pretty boring pretty fast. Also, it's nonsense.

The idea here is to limit expectations and create and uphold stan-dards and boundaries around values instead.

TOXIC EXTERNAL EXPECTATIONS

One of the most damaging forms of expectations are those generated by external sources—culture, church, family. These are toxic, and if you ingest them they will poison you and your relationship faster than Snow White can say "Such a lovely apple, nom nom!"

Toxic cultural expectations about relationships are everywhere: the friend who asks how you can possibly still be single, as if being in a relationship is everyone's ultimate and only goal in life; the aunt at your family gathering who wants to know when you're going to start a family of your own; the girlfriend who expects her boyfriend to propose because it's been a year already and she's not getting any younger.

It's easy to understand how these expectations unhinge us. They fog up our world. They cloud our judgment. They end relationships.

But fear not! External expectations are only as strong as you allow them to be. You have the power to recognize them and reject them. Remember, you are the hero in this relationship! You just need to be able to recognize them when they show up. Let's look at three of the most common external expectation offenders.

1. Complete Crap

Remember Jerry Maguire saying "You complete me" with the sad puppy-dog face and the desperation in his eyes? How many women watched that, shed a little tear, and said to themselves, "That. That is what I want"?

A LOT.

Millions.

Thanks to Jerry Maguire, women now expect to find a man who thinks he needs a woman to complete him. They expect to hear those words. And if they don't? Well, then, it simply can't be love.

Newsflash: this is nothing but a fast track to codependency.

Expecting your partner to complete you (or be your *everything*) essentially strips you of your own power and responsibility in the relationship. You cannot exist in a healthy, conscious relationship if your expectation is to complete someone else, or for them to complete you. Nope, nope, nope.

2. We Wants the Ring, Precious

Did you catch the *Sex and the City* episode where Aidan goes out and buys Carrie an engagement ring and she finds it while going through his bag and it makes her vomit? At brunch with the girls the next day, she expresses her disappointment and explores the fears that the ring has brought up. It isn't her style. Her boyfriend got it all wrong. Surely this is a sign that he doesn't even know her. He can't be the one!

If this was meant to be satirical, we would have had a laugh, but the problem is that this type of storytelling is everywhere, and we know a number of women who've guzzled this Kool-Aid. To these lovely lasses we'd just like to say, *for real?* Are you really going to reduce your entire relationship to a piece of jewelry? Is that what love has become? Honestly, the expectation that the entirety of your unique identity and worth will somehow be expressed by a glorified rock is gross. We have been so manipulated to think that love equals diamonds—the bigger the carat, the bigger the love.

Are they a pretty thing to have?

Absolutely.

Should they be the signifier of an entire relationship?

Do we *really* have to answer that?

3. Love and Marriage

Every day, in countless ways, we are being force-fed the idea that the gold standard of a committed relationship is marriage and all the hoopla that goes along with it. The woman waiting nervously for the proposal; the pressure on the man to make it the absolute best, most memorable, You-Tube-viral-video proposal the world has ever seen! And then there is the size of the wedding, and the dress, and the flowers, and the honeymoon . . . cha-ching, cha-ching, cha-ching. But it doesn't matter what it costs, because we've all been brainwashed into thinking that this, too, is a sign of love.

Don't get us wrong; we have nothing against marriage. We believe everyone has the right to marry if they wish (and we do mean everyone). But does being married prove that you are in a better relationship? You love each other more? Of course not. And by the way, the only thing the cost of a wedding proves is just how deeply we are under the spell of this toxic cultural expectation.

⟨⟨⟩⟩

These kinds of unrealistic and untenable expectations lead to massive relationship disappointments, and they are ubiquitous. It can be difficult to protect yourself and your relationship from the near-constant bombardment. It's time, dear hero, to equip yourself with a sturdy shield.

BOUNDARIES, BABY

Nothing shuts down negative expectations like a good boundary, and if you are struggling with excessive expectations, it's a good sign that you are lacking in boundaries, dear one. If you're living in a world without solid boundaries, it's quite possible you're experiencing any of the following:

- an inability to make decisions without phoning a friend (or five)
- over-the-top dramatic relationships (more on this later)
- an open-book style of communication with anyone who will listen
- a pattern of constantly needing to please others

Do you recognize yourself in any of these examples? If so, congratu-lations! You are one step closer to being free from this misery!

According to Tory Eletto, marriage and family therapist and Insta-gram guru (whom you should definitely be following if you're not already), "Expectations are narratives disguised as boundaries." She further explains that "expectations come from narratives. Boundaries come from values. Expectations create resentment. Boundaries create freedom. Expectations fill the space between you and I. Boundaries hold that space sacred."

Okay, that's a lot of wisdom crunched into a few sentences. Let's unpack that a little by looking at each concept in turn.

We are already pretty familiar with expectations, so we'll start there.

Expectations: *Come from narratives, create resentment, fill the spaces between you and I.*

The narrative driving expectations are those *should* statements we mentioned before. They tell a story with an assumed outcome based on someone else's behavior. Resentment is almost always the outcome. Why? Because we are placing all the power on someone else to do some-thing we want *and* telling ourselves (narrative) that this is how it *should* be done. We don't stop or slow down to question why someone else is doing something a certain way, and we end up filling all the spaces "between you and I" so there is nothing left to explore or learn.

Okay, let's turn to boundaries.

Boundaries: *come from values, create freedom, and hold that space sacred.*

Rather than being rooted in *wants* and *shoulds*, boundaries are rooted in our values. Values such as honesty or kindness. Being able to say *no*, and having that *no* be respected—that's a value too.

Think about what you value. The items on that list represent your boundaries and are the things you need to protect and not compromise. The only way your boundaries are going to be respected is if you are respecting them yourself. If you're not upholding your own values, how can you ever expect anyone else to notice that they are there?

Remember that expectations have to do with the other, and boundaries have to do with the self. It's an expectation if you assume that your boundaries will be upheld without communicating them, or to expect that your partner's boundaries are the same as your own. No two people will ever be completely identical; this idea that we all have to align perfectly when it comes to boundaries is just another fantasy.

The following are examples of how expectations and boundaries play out in a relationship:

- An expectation may be that someone should know exactly what to get you for your birthday. A boundary would be expressing to your partner that gifts are important to you because they are part of your love language and signify that your partner knows you and thinks about you.
- It can go the other way too. Your partner may have the expectation that you should know exactly what it is *they* need. A boundary would be not allowing yourself to feel guilt or a responsibility for someone else's emotional needs, and inviting an open conversation where you can both talk about this expectation.
- If you believe that your partner should always take your side on any issue, that's an expectation. A boundary allows for your partner to have different opinions from your own, and creates space for both of you to discuss those opinions that are important to you without feeling threatened.

Seems pretty obvious at this point that boundaries trump expectations, so why don't we all just naturally operate from this place? Because expectations are formed automatically and unconsciously, whereas boundaries are formed intentionally and consciously—and, quite frankly, that's more work.

The good news is that when you spend time identifying your values and boundaries, you get to figure out the things you're not willing to compromise on. You get to develop, explore, and create boundaries for yourself and your relationships. Most of us try to treat others in the way we want to be treated, but we should be careful not to fall into the trap of thinking that we all want to be treated the same way. An even better practice is to spend some time communicating how you wish to be treated and then listening to what your partner would like in return.

A word to the wise: it's best to get boundaries out in the open early.

When boundaries are clear, the other person in your relationship is never in charge of your happiness or well-being. They can support you, love you, lift you up, and do all of the wonderful things a partner can do, but they alone are not your reason for happiness. This is what freedom in a relationship looks like. And when you don't understand something about your partner, there is no automatic story; there's only curiosity, because you have opened the door to honest conversation. This, too, is freedom. You ask, you explore, you hold the space between the two of you sacred. Allowing that space of unknowingness to exist provides the opportunity for greater trust, honesty, transparency, and vulnerability.

The better to express your boundaries with, my dear!

JUST THE THREE OF US

It takes a level of self-awareness and the expression of boundaries to make a relationship truly work. This is why it's so very important that you go into your relationship with a clear understanding of who *you* are.

A friend of ours once explained the ideal relationship as follows: Think of yourself as a circle—full, complete, whole, and amazing. Think of your partner as another circle, also full, complete, whole, and awesome. To create a true union, you don't combine these circles; you do this:

Your Awesome Relationship

Shared hopes, dreams, wants, desires, family, experiences, interests, etc.

You

Your hopes, dreams, wants, desires, family experience, ambitions, talents, beliefs, boundaries, etc.

Your Partner

Their hopes, dreams, wants, desires, family experiences, ambitions, talents, beliefs, boundaries, etc.

You create a separate circle for your relationship. Within *this* circle are your shared hopes, dreams, wants, desires, family, the trips you'll take together, the life you will explore. You are allowed to stay fully yourself. Your partner is allowed to stay fully themselves. What you work on and build together is in your shared territory: your awesome relationship.

This is why it is critical that you drop your unrealistic expectations but not your boundaries. Whether regarding gift-giving, mind-reading, or when those flowers should be given, your expectations are controlling your relationships with other people more than you may realize. But boundaries—those keep you strong. They'll help you to stay a hero, both for yourself and for your partner. Drop your expectations and you will start to see the other person for who they really are. Hold firm on your boundaries and you'll start to live your true self with another.

CHAPTER 8

WHEN YOU'RE A PRINCE, THEY LET YOU GET AWAY WITH ANYTHING

WE'VE BEEN GUNNING FOR CINDERELLA pretty hard so far, but we did promise this would be an equal-opportunity critique—so watch out, Prince Charming, our sights are set on you and that chiseled chin of yours. That fella, much like his little cartoon lady, is a great big lie, one so utterly ridiculous and transparent that it's hard to believe any of us bought into it in the first place. But we did. Many of us did. Big time. And that ol' Prince Charming schtick—the idea that men need to rescue women and conform to gender roles that are based on a fairy tale—well, it's turning a lot of guys into toads. Don't get us wrong. We're all for good manners and men walking us to our doors. We like those gestures. Love them, even. But we're not so taken with these gestures when they're performative and manipulative. Many men are simply playing the role just long enough to win over the person they want. They are wolves dressed up in Prince Charming's clothing.

TOXIC MASCULINITY AIN'T CHARMING

Toxic masculinity, for those of you who aren't 100 percent familiar with the term, refers to traditional cultural norms around what it means to be a "real man" (i.e., hetero cisgender, obvi!), with a focus on sex, status, and violence that is, well, toxic—for everyone. Within this concept, there are very clear expectations around what men should and shouldn't do when it comes to their relationships. Men shouldn't show emotion (big boys don't cry). Men shouldn't be weak, controlled, or afraid to fight. Men shouldn't hold any power position besides alpha.

What *should* men do in their relationships? (Did you catch the expectation there? Yeah, you did.) This list is pretty sparse: Save. Support. Solve.

This way of being is crammed down men's throats at every turn—through Mafia movies, war movies, crime movies, heist movies . . . really any movie with a bunch of dudes in it. Toxic masculinity saturates the pages of thriller/action fiction, is the standard in sports, and on and on.

Those examples are just the current iterations of this ancient concept. Toxic masculinity has been around as long as fairy tales—much longer, actually. We're talking generations upon generations of men being taught to be tough, to be providers, to win at all costs, to push back when they get pushed, to treat women like conquests, to never talk about their feelings; in short, to be just like Prince Charming. And these expectations are so prevalent that many of us have come to believe that this is just how men are. "Boys will be boys!"

Well, enough! This isn't male nature; this is taught behavior—and it's taught from a very early age.

THE STRONG, SILENT SOCIOPATH

In his book *I Don't Want to Talk About It: Overcoming the Secret Legacy of Male Depression*, psychologist Terrence Real reviews numerous studies on how gender impacts the way we raise our children. "Little boys and little girls start off with similar psychological profiles," he writes. "They are equally emotional, expressive, and dependent, equally desirous of physical affection."

And yet, studies show that from birth, boys are spoken to less and given less nurturing and care than girls—despite the fact that there is ample evidence that in infancy boys and girls display no difference in behavior. Well, actually, we take that back. According to Real, male babies are slightly more sensitive and expressive than female babies. Just not according to their parents. The parents of male babies are more likely to report that their baby is "stronger," while female babies are perceived as being "softer." A University of Sussex research study from 2016 that took a close look at how parents react to babies' cries found that gender stereotyping can start at just three months old.

Whoomp, there it is.

Not to mention the whole "boys wear blue and girls wear pink" phenomenon that doesn't seem to have an expiration date. And gender-reveal parties? Don't even get us started. Thanks for all those forest fires, assholes.

Right out of the starting gate we are projecting assumptions of anger, strength, and independence on half of the human population, essentially raising male children to have less emotional capacity and connection. Maybe this is connected to the fact that the suicide rate for men in the United States is three and a half times higher than that of women, or that men are three times more likely to become alcohol and/or drug dependent. Men make up 93 percent of prisoners in the US penal system, are two times more likely to have rage disorders, and commit 89.5 percent of all murders.

Clearly, the way we've been raising our boys isn't working.

Our society may be evolving in terms of how it handles issues around gender and sex (yes, we still have a long way to go, but we *are* evolving), but many of these toxic male beliefs aren't evolving at the same time. Remember how our childhood beliefs get carried into adulthood and can get up to no good? This is kind of the same thing. Culturally, we continue to saddle men with these outdated ideas and then somehow expect them to grow into human beings who can function in society, solve problems, hold down jobs, get along with friends and coworkers, and maintain an image of manhood that now includes being a loving father and an emotionally available partner. What we are sorely lacking are some role models for all of this. We're still stuck with the charmless Charming. No wonder everything is going to shit.

Carrie Bradshaw was always saying, "I couldn't help but wonder." We're feeling that same vibe, and we have to ask: What is it to be a man, really?

Could it be much simpler and more poetic than it's been made out to be? What if we thought of men as just that: men. Not providers. Not stronger. Not smarter. Not immune to emotional connection or displays of emotion. No need for posturing (or, as we've heard it called, "dick-swinging").

A PEEK INSIDE A PRINCE

Oh, Prince Charming, our nameless vanilla hottie with all those noble intentions. Just like Cinderella, he is a construct, made all the more disturbing because children are the intended target. Let's look at this childhood role model of the masculine ideal, shall we? Mr. All-Style-No-Substance. Strong, tall, proud, heroic, rich, well pedigreed, and classically handsome (oh, and always white), he makes women swoon and leaves men feeling less-than. But what do we *actually* know about the prince himself? Turns out, not a whole lot. We thought it'd be interesting to dive a little deeper into what makes old PC tick.

Here are some observations for your consideration:

- He has no work/life balance. Prince Charming has got to be *on* all the time. Charm don't stop.
- His sole function is to hold power. He maintains his right to that power through single-minded quests that attest to his physical talents and superiority over others. (Well, that *and* nepotism.)
- He believes woman are his to possess—right after he wins them fair and square through a quest.
- He wields all the power in a relationship. He chooses. No one else. Charming, no?
- He clearly doesn't know how to listen to or pay attention to women. Seriously, he couldn't identify his true love by her face; he had to use her damn shoe. That, or he has a serious foot fetish.
- There's a strong chance that he'll age into someone who likes to catfish on Tinder.
- He probably farts a lot. (This observation, courtesy of an eight-year-old.)

Prince Charming is a straight-up dud. We should *soooooo* not be falling for this guy! And we aren't just talking about the cartoon version. Different iterations of this peach of a prince are pervasive throughout our society, and they are casting a collective spell on men and women alike.

Have you ever seen *The Thomas Crown Affair*? Not the OG version from 1968, but the one with Pierce Brosnan and Rene Russo. Brosnan plays a suave Thomas Crown and, let's be real, he is fucking cool. Calm, rich, emotionally unavailable, and—spoiler alert—capable of committing the ultimate art heist without breaking a sweat. He's the kind of guy you'd be 100 percent DTF. Part bad boy, part uptight one-percenter, he flies glider planes, dates supermodels, runs a multibillion-dollar company, lives in a sick townhouse on the Upper East Side, and gives bazillion-dollar necklaces as third-date gifts. Let's be honest: we'd all like to land this lad. And Rene Russo does.

Her character is flown in to solve the ol' Case of the Missing Art mystery. From the start, she knows Crown is the thief. Despite the years of experience that have landed her at the pinnacle of her profession, she kinda just lets that slide. (Cads before careers, ladies!) She's irresistibly attracted to him (duh) and gets off on playing his game—that game where she's his entertainment. She's foxy as hell, guzzles Pepsi One, doesn't like to keep men around (she thinks they make women messy), is smarter than Crown (and he knows it, which makes him all the more attracted to her), and, above all, likes the chase. Doesn't sound like Cinderella, does it? And yet, she falls for his charm, his wit, his rugged good looks, and his thousand-watt smile.

At one point, while sitting on his private beach in the Caribbean, she asks, "You really think there's happily ever after for people like us?"

Oh sure, he's a thief and a liar who's basically an overgrown spoiled brat who thinks he's above the law. And sure, being with him means the end of her life and career as she knows it, but being his one and only special lady is all she desires. Why? Because he's Prince Charming. End of story.

So, whether Prince Charming is coming at you in cartoon form or played by the wildly handsome Pierce Brosnan (we walked right past him on a staircase once in New York City—that man is *fine*), the myth is still just as toxic. It divides the relationship responsibilities between the sexes and places different burdens on men and women—burdens that would be better off shared more equitably.

Ugh, can we just get rid of it already?

Bus driver . . . Move. That. Myth!

DIVIDED WE FALL

The pressure that is placed on men to be strong, to be tough, to be charming, to win—it's getting in the way of men being real, vulnerable, and emotionally available partners. It's also putting a pressure on women that most men are not even aware of.

Melanie Hamlett speaks to this in an article published in *Harper's Bazaar* titled "Men Have No Friends and Women Bear the Burden." For generations, women have been tasked with all the emotional labor of their relationships with almost no acknowledgment of the cost (much like domestic labor). A culture where men have no outlets for intimacy apart from their romantic relationship means that women have to be everything to men.

Hamlett writes, "Unlike women, who are encouraged to foster deep platonic intimacy from a young age, American men—with their puffed-up chests, fist bumps, and awkward side hugs—grow up believing that they should not only behave like stoic robots in front of other men, but that women are the only people they are allowed to turn to for emotional support—if anyone at all."

This is the direct result of that "emotional shortchanging" of male infants that Dr. Real described. Think about it: Have you ever seen two straight men hug? It's painful to watch, isn't it? That shitty back-pat thing is so uncomfortable it might as well be an anti-hug. So, women end up being therapist, lover, mother, sexual partner, *and* best friend. It's a lot. It's too much, to be honest. It breaks women down and it breaks couples up.

WHEN THE NAME OF THE GAME IS SHAME

Women should not be seen solely as victims of the unfair division of responsibilities in a relationship. They, too, are participating in many of the cultural norms around gender roles that result in men being placed under extreme pressure that is often hidden under a mountain of shame. Women frequently complain that they want their men to be softer, more emotionally honest, and vulnerable. But do they? Do they *really*?

According to Brené Brown, the world-renowned researcher on shame, this is not the message most men are receiving from their female partners. In her TED Talk "Listening to Shame," Brown recounts how a man approached her during a book signing and challenged her teachings about vulnerability, saying, "My wife and daughters . . . they'd rather see me die on top of my white horse than watch me fall off. You [women] say you want us [men] to be vulnerable and real, but c'mon. You can't stand it. It makes you sick to see us like that."

He makes a valid point. Many women say they want a sensitive partner, but that often translates to "sensitive to *my* needs, thoughts, and emotions. Don't you *dare* scare me by showing me that you also have them. Someone has to be the strong one in this relationship!" Now, by a show of hands, how many women do you know who've said that they find it a turnoff when a man cries? We know a few. Maybe you are one of them?

Shannon here. It's time for me to share my story of how I got tangled up in the Prince Charming/Cinderella gender fuckery and the toll it took on my relationship. Now, I've already shared that I suffered from a bit of Cinderella Syndrome when it came to my desire to be chosen by a man, but that didn't translate into living a passive life. I've always been fiercely independent and remained so even once I was married. A few years after "I do," I started a successful business, put in the long hours, and began earning more than my husband. I took pride in the fact that I worked throughout my pregnancy, stopped only to give birth, and was back in the office two weeks later (and that was after my second baby)!

I wanted to be the woman who could "have it all," and in many ways, I did. I was able to build a life for my family, we lived in a nice house, and I had a partner who didn't feel pressured or emasculated by my success. And yet, while I told myself that I didn't have a problem with feeling like I was the primary breadwinner for my family, in truth, I had a huge problem with it. I started to feel a tremendous amount of weight (and I lost a lot of weight too). I was stressed out; I drank too much wine (but thought it was okay because everyone called it mommy-juice); and I became resentful and angry with my husband.

I had grown up on a steady diet of fairy tales, and in each one, I was the princess, *not* Prince Charming. This didn't fit my narrative, and so I felt like the "man" in the relationship. And guess what? I started to act like a prince.

I stopped sharing my feelings. I hardened up. I decided that if things were going to be done, they were going to be done my way. Truthfully? I became a bit of a monster.

I was the boss at work, and I felt like the boss at home. It was exhausting. And you know what the biggest problem for me was? That it didn't seem to bother my husband one bit that I wore the proverbial pants. I should have seen this as progressive but at the time I resented the fact that I had to leave home to go to work while he didn't, with my little boy screaming for me not to leave. Never mind the fact that my husband worked from home as a successful visual artist, that he was a caring husband, and was—and still is—a fantastic father.

So why was it so hard for me to accept him as different from the men I had been raised to believe in? Why did I feel so much anger toward him when he was supportive in so many other ways?

About a year after we separated, I read an article in *New York Magazine* by Ralph Gardner Jr., titled "Alpha Women, Beta Men." Gardner talked about how even progressive women who never expected their husbands to support them completely (yours truly) also never expected to do all of the heavy lifting. He writes, "As hip and open-minded as they like to think they are, they were, after all, raised on the same fairy tale as the rest of us—the one where Prince Charming comes to the rescue of Sleeping Beauty."

There it was: my story in black and white. It was both liberating and kinda devastating. In truth, our marriage ended for more reasons than this, but to be reminded of just how deep these

beliefs go and how powerful a force they are on our relationships—well, it was a tough but really important lesson.

The point in all of this is that women are participating in expectations that preserve toxic masculinity too. But we aren't blaming you. Just
like we aren't blaming men for not doing their emotional work. (Blame
equals more shame, and that's what we're trying to avoid.) We are asking
you, once again—and now that you know better—to take responsibility
for your part in this nonsensical gender play.

Curtain!

It's time for a new act.

YOU TO THE RESCUE!

How do you rescue yourself and your relationship from the clutches of
Prince Charming? Well, at the risk of sounding like a broken record, go
back to your beliefs and take a long hard look at the gender assumptions
you've been playing into. (Or, perhaps we should say, the gender assumptions that have been playing you!)

Do you believe that real men don't cry?

Do you believe that men can't show emotion because it's a sign of
weakness?

Do you believe you need to be rescued? And if so, why?

What do you really expect from your partner when it comes to emotional honesty and vulnerability? Because it takes a strong partner to
handle another person's vulnerability.

These questions can be kind of scary, but know this: once you are
aware of the answers, you will possess the power to choose differently.

That's it.

It's really not magic; it's just choice.

You really *can* choose to play any role you wish in your relationship. Maybe you'll even embrace the Cinderella/Prince Charming thing. That's totally okay. As long as it is a *conscious* choice.

We keep coming back to unconscious beliefs and conscious choice because one is your kryptonite and the other, your superpower.

Your unconscious beliefs are holding you back; your choices will set you free.

And knowing that—that's the stuff that makes a hero.

CHAPTER 9

SAVE THE DRAMA FOR YOUR (FAIRY) GOD-MOMMA!

Alright, drama queens, this chapter is for you!

You know who you are.

You're the ones who like to pick the fights and then respond with the silent treatment. When asked what's wrong, you say "NOTHING!" even though that's clearly not the case. You probably follow this by slamming doors and saying shitty things in the heat of the moment that you wish you could take back but *can't*! You are the proclaimer of dramatic lines like: "Now that I see your lies, I've found my truth!" because—BOOM!—the mic-drop on that one is just too tempting to resist.

Maybe your flavor of drama is more the codependence variety. Like when your partner says they can't see you because they have to work and you immediately take this to mean that they don't care about you anymore. Perhaps you're the girl or guy who freaks out if you don't hear back from your partner after a text sent a couple of hours ago and follow up with a "HELLO????" and the pointy-finger emoji.

Maybe you justify all this drama because somewhere along the way you read that book *Why Men Love Bitches,* or you've been told "that's normal, he's gay." So now you believe that this type of behavior is somehow socially acceptable, cute, part of your charm? Queen, please. It's time to break free from the dramaz. Period.

Now, just in case you're one of those Drama Divas in Denial and don't know that this chapter is about you, we've put together a little quiz. You're welcome.

HOW TO TELL IF YOU'RE A DRAMA QUEEN

Answer the following questions with a yes or no.

1. **You consider "Sweet but Psycho" your theme song.**
   Just so we're clear, that song is a tongue-in-cheek cautionary tale, not an actual call to arms.

2. **You use the phrase/have a sticker/own a shirt that says, "I don't do drama."**
   Mmmm-hmmm. Sure you don't.

3. **You think *everyone* around you is super dramatic, except you.**
   Except that you are the only common link between all of these dramatic people. So . . .

4. **"PAY ATTENTION TO ME" is a phrase that you say out loud or in your mind. A lot.**
   If you need a lot of attention, there may be a chance that you do dramatic things to get it. Like saying "PAY ATTENTION TO ME" out loud.

5. You *love* gossip.

   It's fun to spill the tea, but the downside is that it makes people trust you less. If you talk behind everyone's back, at some point it will be behind theirs.

6. You think people on reality television are acting appropriately.

   Those people are getting prompted AND paid to dump a drink on someone's head. What's your excuse?

7. You complain about everything. Like, everything.

   We all go through shit, and sometimes you have a right to complain, but if you're a constant Debbie Downer, it might be time to shift the focus to what's going right, not wrong.

8. You're the one in your friend group that is the automatic go-to for any dramatic situation.

   We fully support being a good friend, but that's different from becoming way too invested in other people's drama.

9. You regularly get into fights with your friends, and you are almost never the first to apologize.

   Best beware, folks can only put up with those antics for so long.

10. You had a super-dramatic parent who likely drove you nuts!

    But you also learned that this type of behavior is normal or expected. Guess what? It's not. You are now as annoying to others as your parent was to you.

11. You've made up something scary to manipulate someone.

    We've heard of people pretending to be pregnant, sick, or threatening to harm themselves just to keep a partner from leaving the relationship. That's ALL kinds of fucked up.

12. **You like to update your relationship status constantly.**
    This screams of self-importance. For sure, your friends want to see you happy, but no one really cares that much if you met someone last week and are now "in a relationship" until the week after, when you change it back to "single" and then talk about it in a public forum with anyone who will pay attention. Maybe chill.

13. **"I'M FINE" is your conflict response at all times—until you release a torrent of obscenities on whomever you're upset with.**
    Trust us, it's time to grow up and be responsible for your own emotional state.

14. **You're always attracted to the "bad boy" or the "player."**
    Because that always turns out well.

15. **You say things like "Don't let the haters dim your shine."**
    People have to have strong feelings about you to hate you. How important do you think you are to people who barely know you? Also, if that many people do hate you, maybe you should look at that.

16. **You post half-naked suggestively posed pictures of yourself on social media accompanied by inspirational quotes like "Prayer is the cure for a confused mind, a weary soul, and a broken heart."**
    What's prayer got to do with your titties?

If you answered yes to any of the above, your results are in: you need to dial it down.

Drama doesn't serve anyone. Not you. Not your partner. Not your friends. Not your coworkers. Not your dry cleaner. Yet there are many of us who truly believe that it ain't love without the drama, and that belief is causing us to act like a bunch of queens with a capital *Q*. But why?

Why do we stir the pot, pick the fights, push the buttons, and thirst for more? It comes back to (ta-da!) your beliefs and the ways you learned to express them.

Knowing that drama stems from your beliefs is a good starting point, but it's not the solution. The problem, of course, is that drama is a hangry beast. Until you can find ways to stop feeding it, you'll spend most of your time enslaved to its hunger pangs. So, we are going to examine three of the most common manifestations of drama and the belief systems that fuel them so you can better understand, and control, your own drama.

1. LADIES AND GENTLEMEN, CAN I HAVE YOUR ATTENTION, PLEASE?

We know someone, we'll call him Drama David, who just thrives on drama. This guy lives for it. Lies for it. Loves to ensnare people in it. He will even go online and self-publish articles for the sole purpose of stirring up attention, DMs, support, a sense of purpose—a.k.a. more drama. He's a high-strung fella who only seems calm when he's sitting in the middle of a shitstorm that he created. It's almost as if drama is his drug, providing him with an injection of attention. But as soon as the high fades, he immediately has to find a way to score another hit of that sweet delicious "OMFG CAN YOU BELIEVE HE SAID THAT?"

The need for attention is the number one reason people engage in drama, and it usually stems from a lack of self-esteem and is a way to generate a sense of self-worth. These types of drama queens are chasing constant external attention in order to validate their existence. (I tweet just to know I'm alive . . . .) In essence, they are managing the terrifying vacuum of their empty inner space. Drama is the coping mechanism, but the belief system fueling this ride is that they need to be seen in order to matter, and this belief is always linked to childhood and different ways of not being truly seen during those formative years.

The need to be seen and loved for who we really are is a base need for we *Homo sapiens*. Maybe we had parents who couldn't accept us for who we are, or siblings we were constantly being compared to. Or maybe we had to compete for our parents' attention. These are all situations that create a drive for attention. And as any kid (or Hollywood celeb) knows, negative attention is better than no attention.

Little kids are great at this. They pick fights and create drama just to be noticed. On the playground. At home. It's exasperating to deal with as a parent and just as exasperating to deal with in adults. We've already learned that the relationship skills we develop as children inform our relationship skills when we're grown. If you were throwing Oscar-worthy performances when young to garner a bit of attention, you're likely doing the same to your romantic partner today.

The next time you're in a fight, you might want to ask yourself, "Is this about needing attention? More important, is this drama solving or contributing to my or my partner's overall growth, or is it holding us back?"

Because no relationship will ever, *ever*, be able to fill the empty hole inside. Only you can do that.

2. YOU CAN'T ALWAYS GET WHAT YOU WANT

You may also use drama in your relationships as a tactic for getting what you want. Take crying, for example. Have you ever been given the advice to try crying if you need to bend someone to your will? This is a classic drama move. Instead of engaging in purposeful and meaningful conversation, you use the waterworks as a shortcut to getting what you want. It may help in the short term, but the trouble is that the long game won't be won with tears or performance. If you really want to achieve a full-bodied partnership, you need to cut the act and get to the root of what's actually happening. Remember, relationships are about growth, not just getting whatever you want whenever you want it as "proof" that you are loved. That's an outdated relationship belief if there ever was one. If you are manipulating drama in this way, you need to pay attention ASAP. You're operating on two-year-old logic, and any chance at a healthy adult relationship is doomed unless you commit to some growth in this area.

3. DANCING WITH THE DEVIL

Sometimes drama is wielded in a relationship for the sole purpose of keeping the other person entangled. This kind of drama comes from a core belief that you cannot be loved and that eventually everyone is going to leave you. So, at the very first sign of discord, rather than getting curious about the space between each other, the drama queen immediately fills that scary space with drama. ("Don't wanna know your perspective because it can only be bad!")

Drama of this nature includes fights full of baseless allegations, smears on character, and lots of attacks. Why? Because as long as the other person is defending, explaining, clarifying, they are still in the dance with you.

This is a crazy-maker.

If you are dating one of these drama queens, stop dancing. Walk away. You will never, *ever* be able to make the person believe you or see your perspective on things. That's the whole point. This is how they are keeping you hooked.

And if this is you: dude, please get some therapy.

HOW TO BREAK UP WITH DRAMA

As we've seen from the examples above, no matter what type of drama you or your partner are bringing into the relationship, it is serving a purpose and is deeply rooted in old beliefs, which can make it a difficult habit to break. Identifying the nature of the drama and the beliefs that are driving it is great, but it's only half the battle.

You will also need some practical ways to catch your drama in the act so that you can choose a different way of being. We'll outline a few ways to do that below. Drama is essentially a belief-based pattern that feeds off of strong feelings, so these practices will look similar to the material covered in part one. The difference is found in the emphasis on adapting this practice for application within a relationship.

We'll start with one of the easiest methods for disrupting drama.

Watch Your Words

We've already talked about how words are spells. A lot of drama is generated simply by the language we use when defining our relationships or partners. Many people, either jokingly or not, refer to their partner as their "better half."

That right there, that's drama.

This term overdramatizes your partner in relation to your own importance. Better half? Why better? If you lose that half, fall out of love with that half, or if that half falls out of love with you, are you left with only the worst half of yourself? No, of course not. You're left with the same you and all your same shit to sort out—it's just that now you don't have someone to snuggle with. Your partner is not half of you; they are half of *your relationship*.

As we wrote earlier, people like to say that relationships are a 50/50 proposition, but we prefer to say that relationships are 100/100. You own 100 percent of your shit. Your partner owns 100 percent of theirs. And you, as much as you can, give 100 percent in your relationship. Even when it gets messy, or hard, or annoying, you still show up 100 percent ready to be in it. That kind of practical commitment kills drama dead in its tracks.

It's also important to pay attention to the language we use when talking to our partners about who they are to us. Consider the saying "I'd die without you." While it might sound like something out of a love story, language like this can create unintentional and unnecessary drama. Do any of us *really* want to feel the weight of someone's life on our shoulders? Sure, they're just words, but they're heavy with feeling, meaning, and dramatic undertones. Many of us think we want to hear these words, even *need* to hear these words, but that's us under the spell of drama.

Here are a few ways you can swap your drama for more authentic language to describe your feelings:

1. **Instead of saying "I'd die without you," you could say "I'd really miss you if I lost you."**
   Seriously, you don't need to start planning your funeral just in case things go sideways.

2. **Try saying "I choose you" instead of "I need you."**
   You need *to pee after that third margarita. You* choose *to let someone into your life.*

3. **"You're my whole world." Swap this for "You're the best part of my day and I love sharing my life with you."**
   Seriously, if they are *your whole world, you need to pick up some hobbies. ASAP.*

If you've somehow mistaken drama for love, you can start proactively changing your language today to something healthier, something that is rooted in growth and not mired in theatrics. This is a lot like the thought-swap practice we outlined in chapter 4. Subtle changes in language will allow you to stay in conscious control and in realistic and real connection. The goal is to keep the whole circle of you intact. Saying or believing in spells like "I can't live without you" will lead you into the dark forest of dependency, where drama lurks in the shadows and a loss of self is inevitable.

Beau here. I'm going to practice some vulnerability (take *that*, toxic masculinity) by sharing a very personal story about how it felt to be on the receiving end of these types of words.

I was in a relationship for two years with a man I loved deeply. He was intelligent, thoughtful, romantic—and he had totally bought into the fairy tale that drama/passion equals true love. He loved to share his grandiose romantic fantasies, which included our lavish wedding followed by our happily ever after. He was fond of sweeping statements like "You're my everything!" and "I'd do anything for you." This included a willingness to uproot his life in another country (that he loved) to start all over again with me, if I just said the word.

Here's the problem with this: as much as I loved him, carrying all the responsibility for every part of his life and happiness weighed heavily on me. Another problem was that if I didn't reciprocate his larger-than-life sentiments, it must mean I didn't love him as much. Right? So, it was hard not to feel like a terrible person. In short, his dramatic declarations of all-or-nothing love left no space for me to have my own reactions. Drama filled all the space between us, and I was suffocating—and feeling like shit for it.

But I was also determined to be responsible for the feelings I was having and to be as honest as possible, as this is one of my core values and therefore an important boundary. He knew that I didn't believe that people needed to be married to be in a happy and devoted relationship, and so every time he asked, "Don't you want to marry me?" (he asked a lot), my commitment to honesty meant that I could only ever answer with "Maybe one day."

I was very clear that I loved him, wanted to be with him, and wanted to figure out a future together. But my practical request to spend more time in a shared space before deciding to move across the world did not align with the passionate, impulsive, ride-or-die-for-love statements that he wanted from me.

I was incredibly sad when the relationship ended, but I also knew that I'd grown in my capacity for honesty, for holding on to my own self-worth while loving another, for not allowing drama to swallow me alive, and in learning when to let go for the betterment of both people—even when love was still there. I also learned firsthand how it feels to be on the receiving end of drama dressed in love's clothing, and it helped me develop into an even more compassionate and authentic partner. It all comes back to love being a practice and a never-ending journey.

Neutralize Drama

Drama is fueled by feelings—a lot of big feelings. So, one of the ways we neutralize drama is by addressing the feelings that arise during the instances when you might normally launch into drama.

A quick review: We are meaning-making machines. About everything. Even though all events are intrinsically neutral, we create and assign meaning based on our belief system and, here we go . . . beliefs drive thoughts, thoughts drive feelings, and feelings drive drama. (Oh! Surprise twist! Bet you didn't see that coming.)

Let's say you've just had a fight with your partner. If you are a human, this will trigger an automatic reaction: you will examine this conflict and assign a meaning that will confirm your deepest fear-based beliefs. When you do this unconsciously, you take neutral events and make them meaningful—just probably not in the ways that might be best suited to actually getting what you and your partner both want.

Here's a tip for how to stop assigning automatic meaning and kick drama to the curb: the next time you feel like throwing a raging fit or making a mountain out of a molehill, try to remove yourself from the situation and remind yourself that it is a neutral event. Sounds easy, but it's not. It's going to take a bit (okay, maybe a lot) of effort to do this, particularly if drama is your scene. The goal is to remove yourself from your emotional reaction so you can work through the conflict without kicking into drama overdrive.

Let's start with that example of your partner not texting you back right away. Instead of going for the jugular with your response, take a step back and think about why they might not be responding to you (that doesn't involve you spiraling into thinking they no longer love you).

Maybe they need a break from their phone.

Maybe it's a hectic day at work.

Maybe they don't know you need that snap reply because you've never communicated that to them.

Listing options is a great way to avoid drama and assigning automatic meaning to a neutral event; it takes away the singular focus of your dramatic behavior and allows you to rationalize and become more pragmatic about situations. A failure to reply right away doesn't signal that they won't go to the moon and back for you, but it might be a signal *to you* that you're assigning too much importance to something that's completely neutral.

The practice of listing options also provides a gateway to examining your beliefs. If you believe that a slow text reply means your significant other doesn't care about you anymore, dig a little deeper and ask yourself where that feeling is coming from. You might find that the drama can actually point you down a path of self-discovery.

Press Pause

Another tool for avoiding drama is to simply take a break. When you feel things are getting heated or heading into Best Supporting Actress territory, politely ask to pause.

In an article titled "Nine Types of Relationship Drama You're Too Old For," dating coach Pearl Flax suggests waiting at least twenty minutes to react, as this is the minimum amount of time it takes our brains to reset in stressful situations. You can go for a walk, listen to some music, or talk out your initial feelings with a grounded friend who'll help center you again. Flax says, "Accept the fact that we don't have control over what other people chose to do or not do. We can only control what we do and how we react to situations."

It's on you to be responsible for yourself and do whatever will allow you to dial it down and return to neutral, non-turmoil territory.

The only rule for taking a pause is this: If you ask to press pause you also have to be the person to ask to press play again. Failure to do this will just mean avoiding the conflict or the situation, which will lead you right back to the drama. So, remember, when you ask to cut, you have to be prepared to say "Action!"

BOUNDARIES (AGAIN)

In chapter 7, we learned that boundaries keep expectations at bay. Boundaries also shield us from incoming drama—as seen in Beau's story above. They also keep our own drama in check. People who enter relationships without solid boundaries tend to attract drama. Without adequate barriers between them and their partner, it's easy to feel completely out of control. This is especially true of those individuals who use drama in order to get what they want. In their minds, drama is about controlling the person with whom they are enmeshed. In reality, people without boundaries have almost no control over their lives because their well-being is tied up in the actions and behavior of another person. This is what is known as a lose-lose situation.

A lack of boundaries can also make it difficult for you to say no even when you want to, which can lead to some serious drama. Maybe you can relate to this. Perhaps you are someone who ends up saying yes to everyone all the time because your boundaries are, well, nonexistent. So, here you are, the yes-person taking on way too much responsibility for other people and then crying to your partner about how stressed you are, and how you can never get ahead, and why does this always happen to you?

Well—tough love alert!—it happens because you keeping saying yes when you want to say no. Your lack of boundaries is setting you up for stress and is generating all of that complaining and drama that you're dumping on your partner. If you want to ditch the drama, just start saying no. Other people do it all the time. You'll be amazed by how empowered you'll feel and how much more space and time you'll have to actually enjoy your life.

Boundaries and self-esteem are intertwined. When you free yourself from being something you believed you need to be and start being who you are and expressing yourself through communication and boundaries, things will start to fall into place as if by magic.

This drama look? This isn't you. This isn't even close to the awesomeness that you are. This is just a result of some bad spells that were cast when you were young. Stop turning a prick of the finger into a bloodbath. Cut the drama, and start making room for the hero that lives inside of you.

CHAPTER 10

SPINNING SHIT INTO GOLD

It's the rare bird that relishes conflict. Most of us try to avoid it at all costs. Even poor Cinderella, who probably wished every day that she could smack those awful stepsisters upside the head, dutifully went about her chores without saying boo. One can only imagine how much her prince walked all over her once he whisked her off to her happily ever after. Mrs. P. Charming was so conflict averse and uneducated on how to manage tough situations that she probably just said, "Yes, dear," until the day her resentment led her to have an affair with the stable boy. Or so we imagine. Impossible to know since all fairy tales lock any hints of less-than-domestic-bliss firmly behind the royal gates, leaving us on our own to figure out conflict in a relationship.

Conflict is uncomfortable, unnerving, upsetting, and, in relationships, inevitable. Conflict is also necessary, healthy, and an incredible gateway to an opportunity for growth. Too bad so many of us are afraid of it and will do almost anything to avoid it.

Unfortunately, cowering from conflict is never a solution, and it's helpful to remember that inaction is still a choice—one that has damaging consequences for you and your relationship. We're talking to you, the person who thinks that not engaging means you're being the bigger person, or somehow lets you off the hook. Maybe you even tell yourself, "Not fighting back makes me the good guy." Wrong. The person who doesn't push back, engage in the fight, or learn from it is the person who never grows up—also known as Peter Pan. Furthermore, every time you choose to turn away from relationship conflict, you send a clear signal to your partner that the relationship isn't worth the effort and neither are they. Over time, avoiding conflict will kill your relationship like a slow-acting poisoned apple.

Conflict is normal. It's wildly unrealistic to expect that two people who get along like peas and carrots are not going to have things that irk each other (like which way the toilet-paper roll goes—which, by the way, is with the paper coming over the top of the roll, not under it). As two people with separate identities, histories, beliefs, and preferences, there's a lot to talk about when it comes to sharing a life together, and there's no fantasy world on earth where those two people are going to see eye to eye on everything. Yet so many of us are brought up with the idea that conflict is a bad thing.

Like so many of our core relational beliefs, our understanding of conflict is largely developed by our parental modeling (especially since we live in a culture that encourages families to hide their conflicts behind their own castle walls). Maybe we saw our parents rage at each other, screaming and fighting, or maybe we didn't see our parents argue or fight at all. Whatever the scenario, it's pretty clear that most of us in Western society have no idea how to have healthy negotiations that aren't triggering, heart-racing, and upsetting, particularly when the person we're arguing with is the person we lean on the most.

Let's explore an example we've all experienced in one way or another. Picture yourself arriving home after a long, exhausting day. You're already feeling irritable and overworked, and you walk into your home just wanting to relax. But what's the first thing you see? The *one thing* you asked your partner to do this morning is still sitting there undone, and then, the next thing you know, you are losing your goddamn mind. "WHY DIDN'T YOU TAKE OUT THE FUCKING TRASH?" you shout, tears welling up in your eyes (which are shooting daggers at your befuddled partner, who's looking at you like you're a dangerous animal that's escaped from the zoo up the road). This just ratchets up your rage. How dare they be confused about what is clearly going on! And now you're in a massive fight and you haven't even taken off your coat. Here's the thing, though: Your partner's confusion is valid, and we'd like to gently suggest that you also may be confused about what is actually going on here.

"And-then-I-snapped" fights are not the product of something our partner has or hasn't done. They result when we haven't put in the work to figure out what's actually upsetting us and why. In that vulnerable moment, stressed and tired, you assign meaning to the trash that's sitting there. The trash is neutral. It's just trash. But maybe you interpreted that trash as evidence that your partner doesn't care enough about you to respect even the smallest request. And that makes you feel like your relationship isn't equitable. Maybe having an equitable relationship is really important to you, for any number of reasons. But over there, in the opposite corner of the ring, is your poor partner, who does not equate the garbage to equality and can't read your mind. When you come out swinging, they are going to defend themselves and very likely react with their own issues. Possibly around feeling attacked or treated like they are a fuck-up over the smallest thing (because maybe they were made to feel like one as a kid). But if everyone could just take a step back, take a breath, and get some perspective on what's going down, it would almost be sort of funny, right? Like, it's TRASH.

When we asked transformational leader Lisa Kalmin about how to handle conflicts in relationships, she told us, "The question to ask yourself is, what is really bugging you? Most of our emotions about an event are not actually about *that* event." Reminder: every event is in actuality a neutral event, except for the meaning we assign it.

Shannon here. I have a great example of this process that I can share with you. I only recently realized why I find arguments with a partner so difficult and why I prefer to avoid them. When I was growing up, my dad was a university professor, which came with some unique perks. For one, I had a great resource for essays, term papers, and homework, but with that help came the feeling that I was sometimes as much my father's student as I was his daughter. If I wasn't able to grasp a concept or a correction, I felt like I was letting him down. I wanted to be his best student, the star of the class. As a result, I found his feedback very hard to hear, even though it was always delivered gently and with love. Still, whenever he told me my work could be better, it would crush me a little inside. (I couldn't see it at the time, but he was obviously trying to help me, and I'm so grateful for that, because without him showing me how powerful my words could be, I doubt I would have had the courage to cowrite this book.)

Fast-forward to my adult life and I can see a history of feeling gutted by male criticism, especially when it comes from a romantic partner (some of it warranted, some not). Recently, I started to get curious about why I find criticism from someone I love so triggering. I dug around a bit inside myself and, boom, there it was. I was projecting the fear of not living up to my dad's expectations onto my partner. These old insecurities and fears were leading me to avoid arguments or get defensive in my relationships. It wasn't until my last relationship that I was able to take those criticisms and observations and use them to create opportunities for growth. Once I started to get curious, I was able to start to become a better version of myself, both inside and outside of a relationship.

Every conflict is a chance for you to understand yourself—and your partner—better. Once you wrap your mind around that, conflict becomes a lot less frightening, and you'll start to experience what a powerful tool it is for growing love. Of course, that's not always easy. Conflict is one of those things that triggers our past bullshit very acutely and very quickly. But healthy people in healthy relationships communicate and resolve. Negotiating conflict in a responsible way, with an awareness of what the core issues actually are—all while being observant and vulnerable enough to actually discuss it—that will go a long way toward sustaining love. Plus, when you are able to understand your partner's actions and reactions, you won't have to make up a story about it. Love is understanding. Conflict is a part of love. Let's get busy understanding conflict so we can begin to work with it, not avoid it.

BRAIN GO BOOM

On a biological level, there is a lot going on in our brains when we experience conflict. Our primary response is to perceive conflict as a life-or-death threat. Unfortunately, the area of our brains tasked with threat detection hasn't evolved much over the ages and can't easily distinguish between the loss of a life we are imagining with our partner and the actual loss of our life. The result? Our brains, like Chicken Little, tend to overreact just a smidge. (The sky is falling! The sky is falling!)

According to Dr. Bessel van der Kolk, who discusses these matters in his book *The Body Keeps the Score*, the amygdala part of the brain acts as a "smoke detector." When the amygdala is triggered, our bodies are flooded with chemicals like adrenaline and cortisol, and we shift into fight-or-flight mode as we prepare ourselves physically to tackle the threat.

While our body gears up, the reasoning centers of our mind gear down. In a *Harvard Business Review* article titled "Calming Your Brain During Conflict," mediator and facilitator Diane Musho Hamilton explains: "The active amygdala also immediately shuts down the neural pathway to our prefrontal cortex so we can become disoriented in a heated conversation. Complex decision-making disappears, as does our access to multiple perspectives. As our attention narrows, we find ourselves trapped in the one perspective that makes us feel the most safe: 'I'm right and you're wrong,' even though we ordinarily see more perspectives."

It is only once the body turns off the flight-or-flight response that the system is calm enough for social engagement and it becomes possible to problem-solve. This is a hardwired response, but the good news is that we can actively train ourselves to respond differently. Real growth is possible when our minds can attain the state of social engagement and problem-solving described above. If both people are willing to be open, honest, vulnerable, and mindful of the present—and their own interpretations of it—a common understanding can be found within the mental chaos of conflict. You've heard of "a meeting of the minds"? This is that.

POPULAR PATTERNS

Relationship expert extraordinaire Esther Perel has identified three patterns to conflict. (Welcome, patterns, my old friend.) These conflict patterns are fairly routine, and if you notice yourself participating in any of them, your first step is to shut that shit down.

1. Confirmation Bias

All the way back in chapter 2 we learned how our brain forms a core belief and then spends the rest of its little life collecting evidence to confirm it (he doesn't respect me because he doesn't take out the trash!), all the while completely disregarding any evidence to the contrary. We will literally manufacture situations to confirm our bias so that we can feel a sense of order or control. (And nothing makes us feel less in control than being in a relationship.) We are also prone to attacking anyone who gets in the way of this process, cuing up many a relationship conflict!

2. Character Assassination

This is the ol' trick where we frame our mistakes as contextual and therefore reasonable, but our partner's mistakes are clearly the result of a character flaw. In other words: you're the perfect princess, and your partner is fundamentally fucked up.

3. Always and Never

Here's another one of our greatest hits—this time from chapter 3, on patterns. Toxic *always/never* language is rampant during conflict. "You *never* take the trash out." "Oh, really? Well, you *always* ignore everything else I do around the house!"

Do any of these experiences sound familiar? Good. Now we're getting somewhere. Once you start to notice your negative knee-jerk reactions during conflict, you can choose to operate from a more rational and aware perspective.

Next, we're going to look at some of the top tools, tricks, and tips for negotiating conflict in a way that fosters growth in your relationship while also allowing you to remaining true to yourself and your needs.

EMBRACE THE NEGATIVE AND AMP UP THE EMPATHY

Negativity has a bad rep. It's so . . . negative. Most personal and relationship development advice skews toward keeping things positive, like, all the time. Problem is, we end up lacking the skills to manage negativity. And by negativity, we're not talking about the smack-talking, insulting, or snarky comments that come out a'swinging in a fight; we mean the "tiptoeing around the tough stuff, don't rock the boat" kind of conversations. An inability to manage negative issues is one of the top reasons people avoid the conflicts that they should be addressing in their relationships.

Have you noticed that when we absolutely *have* to talk about something "negative," we've been taught that the only acceptable way to do so is by stuffing it into a compliment sandwich? You know, where you say something positive, slide in the meaty criticism, and then add another compliment on top? Ta-da! Dinner is served. The little negative morsel squished between the fluffy white bread of praise and positivity makes the whole thing more palatable, right?

Ummmmmmm, maybe not.

When we tiptoe around what's really bothering us instead of pro-actively dealing with the facts, we risk downplaying how important the issue is to us and breeding opportunity for a much more serious conflict down the road. If we could all be just a little less afraid of talking about the negative, we'd be a lot better equipped to manage our arguments in a one-and-done fashion.

Chris Voss, former hostage negotiator and author of *Never Split the Difference*, knows a thing or two about resolving conflict. Voss spent twenty-four years at the FBI, eventually becoming lead international kid-napping negotiator. Safe to say, he knows how to manage a high-stakes situation—and he teaches us how to do it too in his book on the power of straightforward negotiation tactics. One of the keys to successful nego-tiation is what he calls "tactical empathy." As Voss explains it: "Tactical empathy is understanding the feelings and mindset of another in the moment, and also hearing what is behind those feelings so you increase your influence in all the moments that follow. It's bringing our attention to both the emotional obstacles and the potential pathways to getting agreement done."

This is where bringing curiosity into conflict will come in handy. When you employ tactical empathy, you immediately shift away from a place of identifying problems and explaining yourself. Instead, you become curious about your partner's underlying beliefs and feelings while being on high alert for potential solutions. Trust us, this is a conflict game changer.

FROM FURIOUS TO CURIOUS

We are always going to instinctively react to conflict from a place of "It's about me." As humans, we are so ridiculously self-absorbed that we think every single thing is about us, even when we logically know that can't possibly be true. During a conflict, when the biological defense mechanism of our brain snaps into place, we go into self-absorption overdrive. And so does our partner.

Tactical empathy is proactive and, as such, is one of the surest ways to interrupt the instant narrative (rant) that goes off in our minds. Getting curious about our partner's narrative allows our mind to shift from a stressed-out defensive position to a place where we can process the conflict as something other than a personal attack and begin to engage in reasoning and true connection. Easier said than done, we know. This can be very difficult in the midst of a conflict scenario, particularly if you're a Type A who just wants to win.

Speaking of Type A's (guilty as charged), we have some of our own special challenges when it comes to conflict. Namely, we need to be right all the time, and this only gets intensified in a conflict. Add this little peccadillo to our brain's biological penchant for short-circuiting at the first sign of a fight, and this is how not taking out the trash instantly morphs into proof that our partner *never* respects us! (Confirmation Bias has joined the party, and she's ready to fuck some shit up!) Before you know it, we are caught up in self-righteous indignation about how we deserve respect; we are going to the ropes on that argument until our partner sees that we are right and agrees with us. Never mind that this person has shown us in a million other ways that they do, in fact, respect us—we can no longer remember or even see that. Besides, this moment isn't about the trash anymore, or even about respect; it's only about being right.

Once you can back off the idea that you have to be right, you'll be able to see the bigger picture. You may even see old patterns that are inhibiting intimacy in your relationships and find some freedom. Actively listening to someone else's perspective in a conflict leads to greater personal growth and relationship intimacy, and it ultimately feels so much better than being right.

HOW TO TALK WHEN YOU FEEL LIKE YELLING

Once you have a better sense of some of the patterns and expectations that rear their heads during your conflicts, you will be able to choose a more proactive and productive way to engage with conflict in your relationship the moment it arises.

We'd like to share one of our favorite conflict strategies with you. Think of it as fight fairy dust. Sprinkle a bit of this into your next argument and you'll be amazed by how things change. Instead of screaming at each other, you'll have an open conversation about whatever's bugging you. It'll be totally awkward and awful, but it'll be worth it!

Here's what we do.

We stay away from saying anything about how we *feel*.

We do this because accusing someone of hurting your feelings isn't actually productive.

First of all, there is not a lot of room for the other person if you are going to make it all about how you feel.

Second, your feelings aren't facts.

Third, feelings are only reactions. You can talk about the reaction or you can talk about what's causing the reaction so you can actually resolve it.

So, instead of telling someone about how their actions/words made us feel, we talk about our experience of the event using phrases like:

- "When you do _____ my experience of you is _____."
- "I have been experiencing anxiety because of _____."
- "The story I am making up about this is _____."

Notice in the second sentence that we are not saying "I am anxious because of you." Not only would that statement make our emotion the central focus, but it would also be loaded with blame. Blaming someone because of how they made you feel doesn't get to the heart of the issue; it just succeeds in making the other person feel shitty. Move beyond that.

Talk about your *experience* of something, not your *feeling* of it. When you do this, you take the attack out of the argument. You open the door for your partner to understand how their actions were experienced without blame attached. You can begin to have real and meaningful conversations. You'll start to see things from your partner's perspective. Chris Voss would be proud.

Remember, your partner should challenge you to see things in a different way. They ought to be an ongoing irritant. We're not saying you should be fighting all the time, but being challenged is a good thing. Challenge is growth. Growth is understanding. Understanding is fucking everything. There is no fixing. There is only healing and growing and choosing.

DON'T SHOW UP IN YOUR SWEATPANTS SELF

Okay, so you are making some different choices around conflict. You're committed to empathy, you're letting go of always having to be right, and you're making more room in your relationship for the other person by sidestepping feelings and sticking to experience. But what do you do when you need to talk about something seriously icky that is just poised to blow up on you no matter what? Avoid it, right? We know. Avoidance is just easier.

Look at Cinderella and the lengths she went to in order to avoid getting into any tussles with her stepsisters. It was easier for her to just do what she was told and go back to her furry friends. The girl must have been losing her mind to be talking to mice and birds the way she was. And that's the thing—avoiding something that's bothering you will eventually make you deranged. At some point, you're going to let it out, and if you leave it for too long, you'll end up letting it out in a big old fight.

Here's a thought: Why not face the icky bits head-on—sooner rather than later? It takes courage to do this. You'll have to channel all your hero strength and show up as the best version of yourself.

We're writing this book in the middle of a global pandemic; we've all been wearing sweatpants for what feels like an eternity. When it comes to the tough conversations, though, we believe that you shouldn't show up in the sweatpants version of yourself. Rather, you need to bring the highest version of you into your potential conflict. Again, you have to choose to do this. You have to take deep breaths, summon all that you have within you to rise above the neural synapses that will strike, and, above all, you need to remain calm.

It takes some prep work to avoid showing up as your Sweatpants Self, but you know how to do this. Amp up the empathy and curiosity and dial down the feelings and blame. You should think long and hard about your partner's emotions and how what you want to say will relate to their needs and expectations. Act like someone you would be proud to listen to. Be better than your fears. Hold yourself accountable and hold your ground, but be open and willing to listen and learn. Treat that convo as if you were going to the ball: with the highest version of yourself on display. (You might even want to actually dress up a bit for this conversation.) When things get heated, remember who you are trying to be. You are trying to be someone who shows up with class, grace, appreciation, patience, and understanding for the person you love. Be you at your finest. There is no better time than this.

THAWING OUT

So far, we've mostly focused on the moments before or during a conflict; we haven't given a lot of attention to what happens between you and your partner after a tough fight. After a fight you generally feel pretty awful, weird, uncomfortable, and just plain awkward. This can go on for days. Sometimes things just slowly thaw out and eventually feel like they've gone back to normal. This is a trick. You need to deal with it. Dealing with the making-up phase of the fight is just as important as getting to the root of the conflict itself. This is the best part of the growth bit, if you allow it to be.

Unfortunately, we've seen too many friends move on from a fight as if nothing ever happened. Three months later they're complaining to us over cocktails about the same shit all over again. If you want to make the fight count, you've got to close the loop. Here are some general guidelines for how to work with the aftermath of a fight:

1. Give some space. Sure, you might want to cling or have your partner tell you everything will be okay, but let's not rely on lip service when what we really want and need is healing. Ask your partner if they need space after a fight, and then give it. Don't worry, they'll come back to you when they're ready.

2. Keep your mind open and use the time to explore. What really caused the fight? What can you learn from it? How can you use this to help you grow? These are all super-awesome questions to ask yourself after a fight.

3. Be prepared to own your shit. If you get to a spot where you realize you were in the wrong, be brave and own it. We like to use the term *asshole* in our apologies. Admitting to someone that you're an asshole takes guts, and it brings the conversation to a place where the other person can feel receptive and open to your apology. "Listen, I realize I acted like a total asshole" is a great opener.

4. When you're ready, give a real apology. (Shannon here: I teach this one to my kids all the time.) A real apology has three parts:

    a. The actual apology: "I'm sorry I did _____."

    b. The acknowledgment of what your actions caused: "When I did _____, I feel like you experienced _____. Is that what's true for you?" Confirm their experience, and acknowledge it with them. Don't assume.

    c. The vow to be better, which gives your partner a sense of understanding and acceptance: "In the future I will be sure to _____." Be sure to include language you've heard your partner share with you. This shows you are listening.

5. Don't always go for the physical. Some of us think that making up after a fight means makeup sex. (Shannon here: I definitely don't teach this part to my kids.) This is a shortcut, and you won't get the closure you need to move forward if you don't first follow some of the steps above. There will be plenty of time for makeup sex and, trust us, it'll be way hotter after the air is cleared.

It doesn't really matter what your particular makeup ritual looks like, as long as there's some sort of closure. Simply saying "I'm sorry, I don't like to fight with you" is nice to hear, but it doesn't address what caused the fight or how to learn, grow, and avoid similar situations in the future.

As Lisa Kalmin puts it, "Apologizing for real isn't being automatic about it. You need to really look at the effect it had on the other person, to be connected to that. Don't assume that there was a specific impact."

So, be sure you take the time to really talk about what happened to set off the fight and the experience of the situation from both sides. Not only will this leave you feeling better, it will also set you up for better success and outcomes in future conflicts (because we all know this won't be the last of it).

A note: True conflict resolution ultimately takes two people, and these actions will only work in the long run if both of you are committed to finding your way through conflict. You need to start with bringing your best self, doing your inner work, modeling the behavior you want, and having open discussions about conflict resolution. But in the end, it is possible your partner will not be willing to join you in this. This can lead to a very lopsided relationship in which you end up doing the emotional work for the both of you. (This is often quite gendered and harkens back to the idea of women bearing the emotional labor of a relationship.) If you find yourself with an unwilling partner and butting up against the same problems over and over again, you may need to take a good hard look at whether this relationship is serving your growth or has stalled out.

This can be the most frightening moment of all in a relationship, but don't worry, we have your back.

CHAPTER 11

HAPPILY EVER AFTER IT'S OVER

LET'S STATE THE OBVIOUS: breakups are the absolute worst. They're soul-wrenching, depressing, and painful. Like, *physically* painful. Sometimes your heart actually feels as if it's breaking. Breakups are capable of making you feel like you're living in the Pit of Despair, wondering how you'll ever crawl your way out and feel normal again. Did we mention they're also heavy, awful, confusing, and can make you feel like you're not worthy of a loving and equitable partnership?

Why are they so hard?

It's all a matter of perspective.

Have you ever looked at an ex and thought to yourself, *I really wish we'd ended up together*? Not immediately, mind you (see aforementioned Pit of Despair), but years later, when you're creeping their Insta (come on, we *know* you've done it), do you ever think to yourself that you're still missing out?

Our guess is no. In the moment, a breakup often feels like the world is ending, and yet a couple of years later you can look at that same person and think, *Huh, what was I so attracted to again?*

Like we said, perspective. At their core, breakups are deeply intertwined with grief and fear because they signify the end of the *idea* of something. That idea comes in many shapes and forms: a perfect life, a loving spouse, a person to grow old with. No matter whether you're the breaker-upper or on the receiving end (and let's take a moment to acknowledge that both positions are hard), at the core, it's the idea of the two of you that you lose. That's why, years later, you don't feel the same punch in the gut. The idea has moved on. Or you've had new ideas about what you want and don't, and that old person doesn't fit the new narrative.

People are constantly changing and growing, and this is fundamental to why not all relationships last. Actually, it should be considered a small miracle when people do stay together. Keeping up with your own ideas, beliefs, and passions as well as incorporating another's into your consciousness is incredibly difficult and takes a tremendous amount of patience and growth. And yet, so many of us think that finding a person to love and be with is the battle. No, darlings, the battle is in the keeping, not the finding. And not all battles are meant to be won.

THE BODY/MIND CONNECTION

When relationships end, there is a profound sense of loss. Sometimes, just as we mentioned above, you can experience actual physical pain in your heart. You're not imagining it. This is a real phenomenon called *takotsubo cardiomyopathy*, but you may know it by its more fashionable name: broken heart syndrome. For an article titled "The Science Behind Broken Heart Syndrome," journalist Helen Rumbelow spoke to writer Rosie Green about Green's firsthand experience with broken heart syndrome. As Green describes it, at night she was tormented by anxiety, and by day her brain would be "racing and racing."

Now, we have good news and bad news. Our preference is to get the bad news first, so brace yourself: takosubo cardiomyopathy is the heart's response to an intense emotional or physical experience. The heart's pumping chambers change, affecting the organ's ability to pump blood effectively. The main symptoms are shortness of breath, sudden chest pain, or fainting.

Whoa, that's a lot of bad news, amiright? So, what's the good news? The condition is temporary and usually clears up in two months (at least according to an article from Saint Vincent's Hospital).

There is a range of other physical symptoms that can be linked to a breakup, but we're not looking to the heart as the source of your pain. We're more interested in your mind—your addicted mind, to be more precise. Love is a powerful neurochemical experience. Think of your brain as the world's most advanced chemist, your own personal drug dealer. Every emotion you experience is literally a designer drug flooding your body.

Love can be addictive and, as with any addiction, the withdrawal is brutal. Drug withdrawal occurs because your brain has become dependent on the elevated levels of chemicals it's gotten used to. The same thing happens with a love "addiction." Without the constant surges of activity in the brain brought on by the attention you receive from your partner, and the romantic interactions and thoughts you have during the day, the brain is left shivering and crying. So yeah, you do feel like total shit after a breakup. But you need to be careful because, as with drug addictions, these symptoms serve to increase cravings for the object of the addiction—in this case, romantic love.

Mark Groves talked to us about this. "The biological experience of breakups is very real; it's our neural biology firing off like an addiction," he says. "We see [our ex] in a better vision than they actually were. It's important to honor that process so that when feelings come up, you can say, 'Oh, this is just my neurochemistry.'"

This is why it is so imperative to create some separation between you and your ex after a breakup. According to Groves, "You have to cut the cord. You can't stay in contact. A lot of people say that's mean and I say, 'If your healing is the number one priority and you set boundaries around that then you will heal.' But when we allow people to linger it's codependency, and it's hope, and it's human, and it's totally normal. But normal doesn't work relationally for breakups. We've normalized this idea that you need to be friends with your ex as you're going through it. I don't want to be friends with you." Groves goes on to explain, "People catastrophize and ruminate because it allows them to still experience love. Cut the cord. Lose them. Learn about it. Feel the space that is created there. There's no real easy way to do that."

One final suggestion from the amazing Mark Groves is to put a friend in charge of your post-breakup decisions, at least for a few weeks. Don't do anything without asking them first. Feel like drunk-dialing? Call your friend first and ask if this is a good idea (pssst, it's not). Want to write the world's most romantic love letter? Again, phone a friend. Your brain and your heart don't have the best judgment in those first few weeks. Lean on your best people. That's what they're for.

YOU *CAN* WEATHER THE STORM OF YOUR EMOTIONS

A breakup really is the death of what you thought could be. But unlike with a true death, the idea lives on, and it continues to reside in that other person. They still post photos on social media; they may still interact with your friends; they may even live just down the street from you. There they are, still out in the world, just no longer in yours. This creates a complicated but powerful sort of grief.

And you don't want to forget the fear that is also generated when you lose the idea of your perfect future with this person. Humans are terrible at tolerating uncertainty, and our go-to emotion tends to be fear: fear that we will never love again, fear that we can't have our heart's desire, fear that we will die alone, neglected.

Here's another thing we know about breakups. You can't avoid them, and (more bad news alert) you have to move through the pain of them in order to come out the other side. We wish there was some sort of magic pill you could take to not feel the awfulness of a breakup (no, that tub of Ben & Jerry's doesn't count). We know how much they hurt. We've sobbed on the floor until we found it hard to breathe. We've lain in bed wondering why we should even bother to get up. And we've spent hundreds of hours overanalyzing every little thing, attempting to understand how on earth we ended up there.

What we can tell you is that all of this is necessary in order to heal and to grow into the person that the breakup was designed to make you. We haven't talked a lot about destiny in this book, mostly because we don't believe that any one person is our destiny, even though they may *really* feel like it. But breakups? They *are* your destiny, because there's no way you're going through life without them. At some point, someone is going to let you down, or you're going to let someone down. You're probably going to end up in a story that doesn't have a great ending (and, in some cases, one that has a really, really horrible ending), but it happens to everybody in one way or another at one time or another. You can't live without breakups. In fact, you need them. They are one of the most powerful ways of showing you who you are. It's cruel and ironic that it takes someone leaving you (or you leaving them) for you to find yourself, but that's what a breakup forces you to do. A breakup will compel you to feel, even if you are a master of being numb. A breakup will push you to question your judgment. A breakup will make you revisit what it is that you want and need. So, from here on in, we're not going to refer to it only as a breakup. We're also going to call it an opportunity for a break*through*.

GETTING THROUGH TO THE BREAKTHROUGH

So how do you get to happily ever after it's over? More bad news (sheesh!): you're going to have to sit in the shit. You're going to have to feel every moment of heartache, sadness, despair, madness, social media doomscrolling, and insecurity. And you're going to have to feel it deeply. The way *through* the pain is *in* the pain. It's awful. But there is something worse, and that's avoiding the feeling. Avoidance won't magically make your feelings go away. All you'll manage to do is push those negative feelings into the murky depths of your subconscious, where they'll fester away until you have to write a chapter in a book about breakups, and then suddenly . . . *they're baaaaaaaaack*. All those feelings will surge to the surface and crack you wide open, and you'll spend an afternoon crying about your divorce and every other relationship ending that you never fully processed, all while day-drinking and listening to Mazzy Star on repeat. Hypothetically, of course.

The good news in all of this is that if you're willing to allow your breakup to be a process, you *will* find your way through to the other side, and along the way you will transform that breakup into a breakthrough.

Everyone's path is different, but the following are some milestones to look out for, along with some guidance concerning what you can do at each stage in order to make your own healing and growth a priority.

WHAT ARE YOU MAKING UP ABOUT THIS?

Okay. So you're heartbroken. The first thing you're going to do is acknowledge that you are dealing with some deep grief and fear and be exquisitely gentle on yourself. If you need to lie on the floor and cry a bit longer, by all means do so. But once you've peeled yourself off the floor and your eyes are slightly less swollen from crying, you're going to challenge some of the stories that grief and fear are force-feeding you. You're going to do this by asking yourself what you might be making up about the breakup. And you're also going to ask yourself what you're making up about what that means about you. Remember this from part one? Fun, huh?

Breakups tempt us to examine every single detail of our failed relationship and dissect it into tiny, painful pieces in order to look for clues as to why things ended. When you do this, you'll start to invent reasons for why the breakup happened. These reasons may be internal or external, depending on your nature. If you're someone who's prone to taking on too much responsibility for everything that happens, the reasons you invent might resemble something like this: you weren't funny enough; you didn't always want to have sex; you prioritized your work over your relationship, etc. If you're someone who tends to avoid responsibility for the outcomes in your life, your list might look like this: your partner wasn't serious enough; they always expected sex; they didn't respect how important your work was. Your fault, their fault; it actually doesn't matter because neither is totally true, and no matter how much time you spend obsessively making up causes for the breakup, it won't change the fact that you are now single.

Some of us do this investigative work in an effort to figure out how to get our ex back. Like, if we could just solve the puzzle and show our ex that we know where we went wrong, they will have that "aha" moment we're so desperate for—also known as the "I'm-so-blind-I-should-have -known-you-could-fix-this-and-be-right-for-me" epiphany. But that is not the way. You don't revisit the situations to see how you could have been better in order to get *them* back. You go back to the situations to see how you could have been better to get *you* back. The relationships that end are the ones that are supposed to end. They're meant to be the lessons. There's no changing that, no matter how hard you try to wrap your mind around what went wrong.

There are stories, of course, about people who break up and then magically end up together and ride off into the sunset. We all know at least one couple who keeps breaking up and getting back together again. Over. And over. And over. This is called a cyclical dating relationship, and a study out of Kansas University by Amber Vennum, Rachel Lindstrom, J. Kale Monk, and Rebekah Adams titled "It's Complicated: The Continuity and Correlates of Cycling in Cohabiting and Marital Relationships" discovered that more than one-third of couples who cohabitate, and one-fifth of spouses, have experienced a breakup and renewal in their current relationship. But here's the kicker: that same study found that couples who experienced cycling are also "at greater risk of further cycling and experiencing greater constraints to permanently ending the relationship, greater uncertainty in their relationship's future, and lower satisfaction."

Well, doesn't that sound like fun?

Listen, we love *When Harry Met Sally* too. And we even know someone who was engaged to a person five years ago, split up, and now they're engaged again. Umm, also, Bennifer 2.0? Miracles are possible! The question is, do you really want to be waiting on a miracle? Because they are kind of capricious. Even more important, do you want to get back on the merry-go-round (a ride that literally goes nowhere) with the same person? Of course you don't. So step away from the cyclical thoughts, the made-up stories, and the clinging to the past. It's time to move forward.

THANK YOU, NEXT

You're only human, so while you are processing that ol' breakup, you may decide that you need some distraction.

The only way to get over someone is to get under someone, right?

Here's how this wisdom tends to play out:

You will post a super-cute profile on Hinge and wait for the suitors to message you. And message you they will! They'll ask you all kinds of titillating questions, and you'll distract yourself by swapping info on your favorite taco joints in the city and possibly sharing an innuendo or two. You might even decide to meet up with one of these people, because that'll feel great—someone wanting you when the one person you want doesn't. Ah, the sweet elixir of being desirable. Surely this will be a quick cure!

Except it won't be. You'll spend the entire time poking at your guacamole, feeling awkward as hell, and remembering all the guacamole you ate with your ex. That salty, delicious, creamy guacamole—the one that came with those delectable tortilla chips and that adorable little plastic cup of pico de gallo. Tears will well up in your eyes as you try to swallow this inferior guacamole (even though you're at the exact same place you had guacamole before), and you'll chide yourself for thinking you could just distract it all away. You'll end up right back where you started before you got into a cute dress for this lame date—on the couch, in sweatpants, bingeing on Netflix and Twizzlers. Exactly where you should be.

FACT FROM FICTION

To be clear, the impulse to take some post-breakup time to analyze what happened is not a bad one. It's actually a very important phase of processing your relationship. All we are saying is *pay attention to your thoughts*—because some of us sort through the rubble of our relationships in an attempt to protect ourselves from future breakups. The assumption is that if we can understand *exactly* what went wrong, that level of pain will never be inflicted upon us again. At least until you hear through the grapevine that your ex has a new hottie, and you're right back to ruminating over how you probably got dumped because you asked for too much when you should have kept quiet, or how your ex probably never loved you anyway. And on and on.

There may be a sliver of truth in these mental machinations, or there may not be, but be mindful of drawing sweeping conclusions about the nature of love in the pursuit of false security. This is not the same as taking time to mine for actual insight that may serve you in the future. If you really want to ensure your next relationship is a better one, you need to separate fact from fiction when it comes to your thoughts.

We talked earlier about asking yourself what you are making up about your breakup. Now it's time to apply this skill to your former relationship. It's time to drill down for the facts and also what was true for you. You're embarking on a journey into the depths of your being. It won't always be comfortable, but at least you'll be woke. And just know that not doing the work comes with its own perils. You'll be as hopeless and helpless as Sleeping Beauty if you don't use this opportunity to wake the fuck up about what you want, what you need, and how you'll show up more authentically for the next lucky person who comes your way.

HONEY, YOU CAN LIVE WITHOUT HIM

How exactly do you separate fact from fiction as you start to dissect your relationship? For starters, do *not* make a breakup playlist. Scan the internet and you'll find a lot of websites doling out this type of shit advice. How on earth is making a playlist going to make you feel better? It's basically like inviting Drama over for drinks and expecting her to help in *any* way. She'll just spill red wine on your sofa and vomit in your plant.

We understand wanting to listen to sad music and wallow in your pain, so we'll give you a day. One day. After that, turn it off, for God's sake, and just put on a podcast and learn something while you clean the house. Yes, you heard us. On this one, we're taking a page from Cinderella and advising you to start cleaning. Mopping. Vacuuming. Doing ten loads of laundry. Scrubbing the toilet bowl.

Why are we telling you to do this?

Well, for one, being sad *and* living in a dirty house is just plain depressing. But don't just take our word for it. Dr. Rebecca Beaton, founder and director of the Anxiety & Stress Management Institute in Atlanta, Georgia, encourages her clients to use cleaning as a therapeutic task. "Cleaning up our external environment can make us feel like we're cleaning up our psyche," Beaton says. So, we say it too: Clean, clean,

clean. Clean your junk drawer and toss the letters and cards your former partner wrote to you. It's a two-for-one bonus: you clear out the junk in your head and your heart at the same time. While you're at it, toss out all the shitty stuff you're telling yourself—such as you'll never find anyone that great again, or how traveling without them will be so sad and lonely. Nope. Hit it with a spray of Lysol and scrub that sludge away.

FUN WITH FEELINGS

Now that you're up and about, how about some fun games to further assist with processing some of these big feelings you've been having. We're circling back to that whole "feelings aren't facts" thing again. For example, the feeling that you'll never be happy again isn't actually a fact, but it can be hard to remember that. But you *need* to remember this, because during a breakup, understanding that feelings aren't facts is a critical part of the process.

We find it helps to write down all of our feelings and see if we can actually turn them into facts. For example, we might be feeling really lonely, but the fact is that we have a lot of great friends who are around to support and love us through this process. Or we might be feeling like we'll never fall in love again, but the fact is that we've been in and out of love more than once in our lives, and we've got plenty more love to give and to receive.

Go ahead and try it for yourself.

Get a piece of paper and divide it down the middle to make two columns. Label the first column *Feeling* and the second column *Fact*. In the *Feeling* column you might write something like "I'll never find anyone else who can love me that way," and in the *Fact* column you'd write "There is ample love and opportunity out there in the world for me." When you start this exercise, you might be shocked by how many of your feelings do not line up with actual facts (hint: most of them).

Here's another fun exercise to try. Let's create two labels and break them into columns again. In the first column, write down all the things your ex seemed to be in the beginning of the relationship; in the second column, list how they actually were when you look back on it. For example, maybe you thought they were protective and wanted to spend time with you, but looking back you notice that they were actually possessive and wanted to monopolize all of your time. Or perhaps they appeared to be romantic (great!) but in actuality were not connected to reality in a way that served your relationship (it's not so romantic if it's not real, right?).

This is not an exercise designed to villainize your ex. What you are doing here is separating fantasy from reality. Breakups are excellent at nurturing fantasy, and all those post-breakup feelings can lead to you rewriting your relationship after the fact. You may find yourself thinking, *He only cheated on me that one time; he can't be so bad*, but once you start identifying and listing the realities of the situation, it becomes easier to spot the red flags all over your former red-hot love. It's okay. This is why it ended. Move through it.

One last list (really, you're getting so good at them!): try writing out all of the things you want in a partner, and then check off the ones that your former flame provided. You might be surprised at the gaps. Mark Groves told us that when people create this list, most realize they've been settling for somewhere between 20 and 50 percent of what they wanted.

Nobody is perfect, but seeing a list of things you wanted but didn't actually get allows you to see the reality of your relationship. The added beauty of making all of these lists is that you'll gain greater clarity around precisely what you want and need in your next relationship and what you weren't getting in your last one. This is progress, and this is what transforms your breakups into breakthroughs.

This isn't just lip service. Both of us have been through devastating, heart-wrenching breakups while writing this book. As if living through a pandemic wasn't hard enough, we also had to suffer the indignities of ending our relationships/marriage while writing a book about relationships! (Yes, we have discussed the irony of it all ad nauseam, thank you for asking.)

The silver lining was that we got busy putting into practice all of these techniques, and they really do help. There's no magic bullet when it comes to getting through your heartache. Time does heal. Although, when it comes to healing from heartbreak, time seems to move in slooooow motion. As you pass through those endless days of feeling like your heart has been punched out of your body, the act of committing to learning and moving forward really does wonders. Add to that the knowledge that you are doing this hard work because you honor your own growth and healing, and because you believe in a life where you get to design and choose the relationship that is right for you—it helps to remember that too.

Finally, try to remember that it will get better.

Trust us.

TAKE A CLEANSING BREATH

You've been processing your thoughts, cleaning up your space, and writing your lists, and now it's time to bring your body on board. Earlier in the book, we mentioned that thoughts are the domain of the mind, and feelings are the domain of the body. Alongside grief and fear, plenty of other big feelings show up during a breakup, and we've looked at how they have the power to physically knock you onto your ass from time to time. Here's the thing about emotions: you can handle them. Emotions are fluid. They come in and go out, and sometimes the tide is high and the waves are crashing, and other times the waters are calm and still.

The knowledge you can gain from emotions is the payoff for the pain they cause, but processing emotions is not easy work. Without this emotional processing, however, you are very likely to create unhealthy coping mechanisms that specifically target the body (where your emotions reside), such as overeating, binge drinking, or excessive exercise.

We recently tried an interesting meditation and clearing technique suggested by our friend Nada Vignjevic, a Calgary-based life coach who studied under Deepak Chopra. She calls this technique "clearing the weeds," and it can be used for all sorts of emotional events that we may not have processed fully. It works by bringing our thoughts and body together.

Nada suggests meditating for twenty minutes. Much like in the meditation practice we outlined in chapter 4, during these twenty minutes you are simply paying attention to your breath moving in and out. When thoughts come up, you simply release them without judgment and return to your breath. Do this over and over again. We like to make sure we are breathing from our diaphragm during this process and allowing our inhalations and exhalations to be the same length of time. This helps us to reinforce the body/mind connection during our practice.

Once you have finished the twenty minutes of breathing, Nada suggests that you write about something from your past that bothers you. We were shocked by how visceral this process was for us. From this place of centeredness, we were able to engage with memories that were stored in our body along with a great deal of sadness. The freedom we felt when we were able to set the memories and stored emotions free allowed us to heal our bodies and our minds.

TACKLE TRAUMA WITH THERAPY

Traumatic events are stored in the body and mind and, as we've mentioned, breakups often feel similar to experiencing the death of a loved one. Except this particular loved one is still living a life without you. In some cases, this can be traumatic.

Many wellness practitioners and therapists teach that emotions that are not released from the body, especially over a prolonged period of time, can manifest as health problems. This has been backed up by medical research by the Mayo Clinic that shows how long-term stress lowers our immune response, creates inflammation, and interferes with hormone levels in our bodies and brain.

You can make a practice of processing and experiencing your emotions, paying attention to your thoughts, and reaching for better ones, but in the event of trauma, the best way forward is therapy. There are many therapies available, from traditional talk therapy to neuro-linguistic programming to Somatic Experiencing therapy—which is based on the theory that the physical body needs to process trauma in order for it to dissipate properly. Whatever modality most appeals to you, we highly

encourage exploration and reaching out to get help during a breakup—
or anytime you have things to process. You don't have to do this alone.
There are experts in these fields who are here to help people through
difficult times.

WHY SO SORRY?

Okay, so let's say you've spent the past two weeks, or four, or six (we don't
judge), sitting around feeling sad and lonely. But your house is spotless,
you've been meditating, you found yourself a therapist, and you're starting to feel a little better. Maybe it even feels like it's time to get up, put
on some lipstick, and face the world. Good for you! You have reentered
the land of the living.

Victoria Gigante, counselor and cofounder of the Higher Purpose
Project, calls this the "rebuilding phase." In her article "How to Rebuild
After a Break Up," she writes about the importance of allowing this phase
to play out. Rebounds are not the way to go after a long-term relationship breaks down (remember the disastrous guacamole night?). Instead,
Gigante suggests that this is the time to rely on yourself and focus on you.
"As you build up your confidence and regroup, you'll get clearer about
what you want next," she writes. "Some pieces from your past may continue onward, but some may completely change. Be selective about what
you bring along for the ride and trust the process as it unfolds. Don't cling."

A word of warning, though: out in the real world—the one beyond
your couch and your bed—are people who are going to ask questions.
Not your close friends; we're talking about the casual acquaintances, the
friends of friends, and let's not forget the (shudder) friends of your ex.
We don't know about you, but we both grew up in fairly small towns, so
running into an ex or running into a friend of an ex was pretty much a

given. And even if there's very little chance of running into your former flame, you're still going to have to answer that dreaded question: "How's Jack, or Jill, or [insert name of your ex here]?" The answer is that you don't know or even give a flying fuck how they are, but that may not be your best go-to response.

So, what do you say?

Simple.

You tell the truth. "We broke up." End scene.

Don't get into it. Don't start talking about how it came out of the blue or why your ex is such an asshole, or how you've been miserable and this is your first night out and that's why you have a drink in each hand.

In the field of crisis communications, this is referred to as "staying in your swimming lane." This is where you need to be, just casually back-stroking along, and not jumping off the high diving board. Now is not the time to get into the dramatics, the heartache, the pain, or the anger. Rise above, hold your head high, and simply state the facts like the god-damn hero you are.

Shannon here. Here's what will start to happen when you begin to tell people you broke up, got divorced, moved out, etc. You will receive a sad face, most likely followed by something along the lines of "I'm so sorry to hear that." This was the reaction I received about 99 percent of the time when I shared the news about my divorce. I get it; we all react with disappointment when we hear about a breakup because the common assumption is that something has been lost. Divorce is particularly cruel for this. The stigma around getting divorced is real, and negotiating the sea of sympathy from well-meaning people every time I left the house was, at times, more arduous than the divorce itself.

There was the exception of one awesome person who beamed and said "Congratulations!"—which was by far one of the best responses ever. Imagine if we all congratulated each other on being newly single instead of treating each other like we've just been diagnosed with some terminal illness.

I'm not suggesting you go around congratulating everyone who says they've just been dumped—that would be weird. But maybe if we all understood that the end of a relationship also signals a new opportunity to find ourselves again, it might radically change how we react to, process, and move on from a breakup. Just a thought.

Even though breakups are more socially acceptable than ever, it's still hardwired into us that divorce equals failure. But it's not really divorce that's the problem—it's the overall lack of acceptance when it comes to people changing or couples growing apart. When something ends, it's easy to think that it's a tragedy, and those sad faces at parties aren't helping. Also not helping? Those friends who think that trashing your ex is a form of solidarity and support. It isn't. If you are one of those friends, stop doing that.

Navigating family can be particularly difficult during a breakup. Everyone is going to have an opinion, and some family members won't be able to help but share theirs. It's important to remember that while extended family will experience a loss too, you can't allow their feelings and opinions to override your own. You are the priority right now (and your kids, if you have them). You need to take care of yourself and connect to your own feelings and emotions, not those of your sister-in-law, or your parents, or your ex's parents. Be steadfast in your commitment to yourself; it's the only way through the storm.

RECLAIMING THE ME IN WHAT USED TO BE WE

Once you've faced the onslaught of "I'm sorry" and your breakup is out in the world, you'll enter a phase of reclaiming the parts of yourself that were intertwined with your significant other. We are not saying that you need to find yourself again. If you've been following the teachings and keeping yourself whole, it'll be more of a detachment from the relationship than a commitment to finding a brand-new you. Still, some negative self-talk will likely rear its not-so-pretty little head. Even after all the work you've done on yourself, it's worth watching out for things that threaten to suck you back into unhealthy cycles. Given the chance, old thoughts you figured you'd dealt with once and for all will come back to haunt you, *Amityville Horror*-style. That's why it's important to remember that you are still a whole, complete, lovable, and amazing person. This is also why you need to begin reclaiming the awesome parts of yourself that you may have ignored during your relationship. (We get it, it happens.)

How this is achieved will vary from person to person. For some it comes via a yoga retreat; for others it's through taking up a new hobby.

It's important that you take as long as you need to sort through these feelings. We've heard people say ridiculous things, like "It takes half as long as the length of the relationship to get over someone," or "It takes twenty-one days to break a habit." Bollocks! There is no set amount of time for this work and no magic formula. But now is a great time to develop a daily practice if you're not doing one already. That might be something as simple as focusing on feeling just 1 percent better each day. One percent is a small number, but over a week or a month or three months, it can really start to add up.

We recommend a practice of taking a few moments each morning to list everything you're grateful for. Actually, this is a great practice regardless of whether or not you're living in the land of broken hearts. We do this as soon as we wake up. Before checking our phones or getting a cup of coffee, we repeat what we're grateful for a few times over in our minds. It sets a positive tone for the day and reminds us that we have so much to appreciate, even on the days we feel down.

Above all, this rediscovery phase is a time to be a little bit selfish. This is your moment to reconnect with yourself and all that you love about yourself. You are going through a transformation. You are stepping into who you are meant to be, and loving yourself throughout the process is vital. Not because no one else will, but because you need to love yourself before you can truly learn to love someone else again. After all, your relationship with yourself is a gift, one we think can be the greatest love of all.

CHAPTER 12

TRUE SELF-LOVE CONQUERS ALL

THERE'S A LINE IN A Boxer Rebellion song that we really love, about how you can fall if you don't know yourself at all. That's the root of everything, isn't it? It's a beautiful thing to know your needs and your beliefs, your strengths and areas that still need work—and then to have the privilege of sharing these with someone else, maybe for forever and maybe not. We believe that every relationship is a gift. It doesn't need to be permanent for it to be precious. And it doesn't need to be a failure just because it ends. You can choose to make connecting, learning, and growing a part of every stage of your life. This is never dependent on another person because *you* are the constant in your story. You are the one with your hands on the reins. You are the one with the power to choose who enters your story and why.

WHITNEY WAS RIGHT

So many of us are not loving ourselves as much as we would a partner, and we need to start. To love oneself as much as we have loved others may be difficult, but what if we did just that? What if we fell in love with ourselves?

Whitney Houston was right!

Crack *is* whack, *and* learning to love yourself really is the greatest love of all.

Loving ourselves is a journey, and it's one that has peaks and valleys. It requires us to be in a state of constant inquiry with ourselves, asking ourselves some important questions: How am I being? What am I thinking? Can I reach for a better feeling thought than the one I currently have? And how am I showing up—for myself and for others?

This type of loving self-inquiry allows us to move into relationships of our choosing and show up as someone ready to grow and give of ourselves. And when we live in this way, even our breakups can be a gift. Whenever a relationship ends, we have the opportunity to reexamine our relational beliefs and to take an exploratory deep dive into which beliefs are working for us and which are not. We discover that we *can* make it through and still be happy—in some cases, even happier—thanks to the lessons we learned along the way.

If we truly want a life (and love) like this, we must let go of the fairy-tale narrative that tells us there is some sort of happily ever after, because—let's face it—life isn't that damn simple.

Just as loving ourselves takes guts, so too does loving someone else. It takes courage to accept that even your ideal relationship of choice will have its ebbs and flows. Think of them as contractions. Something is being born. It's you!

They say love is blind. But that's only because we haven't been properly taught what to look for. If we knew what to look for within ourselves before looking for someone else, we wouldn't be blind—we'd be free. Free to love. Free to choose. The power is within you. You just need to open your eyes and break the spell.

We started this book with a story about a woman who seemingly had it all but still felt incomplete. Her desire to have a person in her life outweighed all else. Thinking about that #BossBitch now, we like to imagine her a little differently. We picture her enjoying all of her moments in life—the ones alone and the ones spent with a partner. We envision her going on dates, staying true to her values and boundaries, expressing her needs, being curious about her lovers (and, yes, we like the idea of her having a few lovers, not just "The One"), and picking herself back up again when things don't work out. We see her journeying deeply into herself so she can then take journeys with others. We imagine her making some mistakes and choosing the wrong guy from time to time, but we're not worried. She learns from that and chooses differently in order to break her patterns, stand in her power, and own her mistakes so they can contribute to her growth. We believe her to be a strong, independent woman who chooses a relationship but doesn't need one. And that sad-sack singleton she thought she was before? That doesn't even cross her mind anymore. She knows herself now. She knows her shadow sides and her strengths. She knows her limiting beliefs and how to break free of them. And, above all, she isn't afraid to try, and then try and try again. Because she—like us—loves love. She believes in the power of it, in the beauty of all that love and relationships can bring. What she doesn't love is fantasy. She's over it. Officially.

She's our girl, and we believe in her.

We believe in you too.

And we can't wait for you to write your very own happily ever after the fairy tale.

CONCLUSION
CINDERELLA, A TRANSFORMATION

We wrote this book during the COVID-19 pandemic—together but apart.

Many a brainstorming discussion was held late at night or early in the morning, over Zoom, the phone, or text. Before we sign off, we thought we'd share one of our late-night texting sessions in which we imagined what it might be like if our girl Cinderella got her hands on the tools provided in this book!

Beau: Maybe we should end the book by talking about what Cinderella would have been like if she had done the work.

Shannon: LOVE. The idea of her actually being self-aware would be interesting to explore. Should we put her in the present day? Imagine what her life would have been like if she had access to the internet?

Beau: Or our book . . . although then we wouldn't have a book so . . . *Debbie, You Bitch* doesn't have the same ring to it.

Shannon: Or KAREN.

Beau: HAHA. *Karen, You Bitch* is a whole other book about a whole other thing.

Shannon: TRUE! Maybe we should stick to her original setting—her rewrite takes place in a land with princes and castles and balls and such. And she can be the only self-actualized woman in all the kingdom.

Beau: Hmm. So, once upon a time there was this girl named Cinderella. Who had some bitch stepsisters and a raging asshole of a stepmother and an absent father.

Shannon: Does the father still die? Or are we keeping him around as more of a deadbeat for this version?

Beau: I guess he could be a deadbeat dad who doesn't stand up for her even though she's being treated like shit because he had his own mommy issues and was treated like shit by his mother, which is probably why he chose her stepmother to marry so that he could re-enact that childhood trauma without knowing it. Definitely didn't have the balls to stand up to his own mom, and doesn't have them to stand up to his wife even when he sees how she treats Cinderella. That's gotta do something to Cinderella's head, right?

Shannon: Yes! She wants to get out and be with someone strong who can protect her. And she meets the prince! I don't think she can end up with him though.

Beau: Well, how does she start doing the work?

Shannon: Maybe the fairy godmother is her therapist?

Beau: Ha yeah! Her life coach. She's tired of being treated like trash by her sisters but she also kind of feels like she deserves it because in her mind if she didn't her dad would surely have done something to stop it. That's what dads are supposed to do.

Shannon: God, her dad sounds like an asshole.

Beau: But maybe her fairy godmother therapist starts to teach her little things like how to be present and to take time to feel good about her accomplishments even if it's just cleaning the floor really well.

Shannon: LOVE.

Beau: And over time she starts to see herself differently and realizes she has value.

Shannon: And she stands up to her sisters!

Beau: Her confidence grows and she tells her stepsisters to go fuck themselves.

Shannon: Starts to participate in some conflict to break her pattern. I like it.

Beau: And definitely it takes some time but she starts to figure out she's actually a really smart girl. She's great with animals, and she has an amazing imagination, and she can sing too!

Shannon: LOL. Ohhh, maybe the palace hires her to sing at the ball!

Beau: Yes! I love that! And her bitch stepmother tries to keep her from leaving the house by burning the dress she was going to wear, which is a really shit thing to do, but Cindy calls a friend and borrows something cute, because in our story Cinderella isn't a solo being—she takes time to build relationships with other townspeople and farm girls and has a little clique of people she can rely on and trust.

Shannon: Yessss. So, she plays a set at the ball and the prince can't take his eyes off her because she's gorg and has a great voice but also A LADY WITH A JOB?? I mean, at the time, pretty ballsy for a woman to work outside the home.

Beau: Maybe she sings "Independent Women" by Destiny's Child at the ball.

Shannon: Haha. Or "Single Ladies"?

Beau: Naw, that gives way too much importance on belonging to someone else. Look, I have a ring! I've been chosen.

Shannon: Right right. Great song though. God, I love that video. I still wish I could dance like Beyoncé. That class was useless. I think we're getting sidetracked . . .

Beau: Typical of us. Anyway, Cindy sings and the prince comes over to say "hey girl."

Shannon: God, that's his opener?

Beau: Yeah. She rolls her eyes at it too. But she thinks he's a babe so she's willing to overlook it.

Shannon: I get that.

Beau: But you know. Fuck Boy—big red flag #1 ignored.

Shannon: God, why do we never see the red flags until AFTER?

Beau: Because of our confirmation biases. We only see what will confirm our beliefs.

Shannon: DATA DISTORTION!!!

Beau: I'm willing to bet that Princey might be a pretty neglectful boy-friend/husband—always busy, never there, doesn't stand up for her. He's hot but basically he's like her dad except she wants to bone him (the prince not her dad).

Shannon: Thanks for making that clear. So she basically ends up with her dad (but not).

Shannon: Is it bad that once my kids go to bed I eat all their candy because tomorrow they won't remember that they have it?

Shannon: Like I'm stuffing my face with M&M's right now.

Beau: Mmmmmm M&M's.

Beau: But since she's been doing the work, she's a bit more cautious, so when he throws himself at her by tracking her down with a shoe, she thinks that's a bit weird.

Shannon: Yeah, stalker much? But she agrees to go on a second date. And maybe it's on that date where she talks about some of her bound-aries and values.

Beau: Do they go to a tavern? Does she notice him looking at the barmaids?

Shannon: Oh yeah, for sure.

Beau: Do they enjoy a jug of grog? And also, what is grog?

Shannon: I think it's beer? Probably an IPA. She seems like the type of girl who would be cool enough to drink grog. Because SHE likes it. Not because it's what he wants to order.

Beau: What do you think they even talk about? Because as we know, all they did at the ball was stare at each other and became obsessed.

Shannon: LOL. Maybe he's really interested in her story and actually asks questions about her instead of just making it about himself. Because he's into her and he knows he can't just be charming. He's got to be inquisitive too.

Shannon: God I love it when a man asks me questions. So few of them do and I don't understand why.

Beau: Because they are trained to impress so they are just all about themselves all the time.

Shannon: It's exhausting to listen to.

Shannon: I bet the two of them move in together. Wait. Could you do that back then or did you have to be married?

Beau: I think you had to be married. Do you think she dealt well with the pressure of being a princess or was it a Diana moment?

Shannon: Oh, I think she would rise to the occasion. She'd step into her power and become the woman she was meant to be.

Beau: What do you think the sex is like? Is she disappointed, because obviously they didn't bone before marriage back then. LOL.

Beau: Or maybe she never saw a peen before.

Shannon: Hahaha. I bet their sex is fine. But not mind-blowing. The mind-blowing sex doesn't come around very often.

Beau: No. She's saving that for the stable boy. Or the court jester who's not actually that cute but who makes her laugh.

Beau: What do you think life is like now that Cinderella doesn't have to clean anymore? What does she do to pass her days? And though she didn't like being a servant I feel like she took pride in her work because it was all she had. Does she have an identity crisis?

Shannon: I think she becomes an activist for animal rights. Sets up a foundation, makes the castle go fully vegan.

Beau: Haha.

Beau: Every couple has issues. What do you think Cindy and Charmy's are? And how do they work through them? I'm pretty sure Cindy has abandonment issues, and probably a jealousy thing.

Shannon: She's still going to play the victim. A lot. Even though she's working on herself.

Beau: Maybe Charming feels like he will never live up to his father. He worries he's not enough for a girl like Cindy.

Shannon: I like the idea of them both going to see the fairy godmother for couple's therapy.

Beau: How do you think they both act from their subconscious beliefs?

Shannon: I'm guessing that Cindy chooses the prince because deep down she thinks she wants to be taken care of because her father never did that for her. But she finds out that being taken care of doesn't have that many perks when she's home alone in a castle all day, even though she's got her animal rights work going on.

Shannon: And on the prince's side, he's probably always going to feel like he's never going to be enough for her, but he masks it by telling her she doesn't show him enough gratitude for all he does for her, like running a kingdom.

Shannon: So they end up at this spot where he feels like she doesn't appreciate him enough and takes advantage of him and she feels like he doesn't even understand her needs or what she really wants. Then they start sleeping in separate wings of the castle.

Beau: Yup, sounds about right.

Shannon: And they don't know any of this stuff about themselves until they get into a relationship because these are all relational issues.

Beau: So, what do they do about it?

Shannon: My guess? Cindy starts to realize she chose someone from a place of trauma and starts thinking about starting over.

Beau: Does Princey come around and do his work or does she figure out a new life? I guess she's never consciously chosen what she actually wants because she's never really been in a position to do so before.

Shannon: I mean, do we want her to end up with him? Now I like the idea of them working things out.

Beau: I think it's an option. Maybe if they both stop trying to be who they think they should be they can discover who they are together and how that works.

Shannon: I'm still thinking about the stable boy.

Beau: Aren't we all?

Shannon: LOL. That or they can consciously uncouple. Learn more about themselves through the ending of their relationship vs. staying in it just because that's what people are "supposed to do."

Beau: I imagine being royals adds a whole other layer of external expectations.

Shannon: No doubt. Cindy learning that she doesn't need a man appeals to me.

Beau: And maybe she does learn that. And gets to have one anyway. Because when you don't need someone you can enjoy them more.

Shannon: Ha. Very true. Instead of worrying about them leaving you constantly. You get to see them for who they really are, not who they are to you. And just live in that.

Beau: And isn't loving someone really seeing who they are? And loving them as they are while holding space for them to grow into the potential you also see but often they cannot?

Shannon: *Sigh* that's beautiful.

Shannon: And I think also being strong and holding to values and setting bars that you know they can meet even if they think they can't. This sounds like a very growth-based relationship for our two lovers. Maybe THEY write a book!

Beau: Cindy becomes the Brené Brown of a land far far away.

Shannon: Haha. And they go on tour, teaching couples how to be more responsible—for themselves and each other. Maybe they end up fixing the whole fairy-tale narrative. Imagine??

Beau: So basically they are us. LOL. Now that sounds like a happy ending to me.

Beau: AND THEY LIVED AS HAPPILY AS THEY COULD CONSCIOUSLY WITH LOVE AND RESPECT FOR EACH OTHER. THE END.

Shannon: Haha. BOOM.

Shannon: Love you, boo.

Beau: Love you too, bb.

NOTES

INTRODUCTION

p. 3, "Molly, you in danger, girl": Jerry Zucker, dir., *Ghost*, 1990 (United States: Paramount Studios, Howard W. Koch Productions).

CHAPTER 1

p. 14, "The Last Unicorn grossed $6,455,330 at the box office worldwide": "The Last Unicorn (1982)," The Numbers, n.d., www.the-numbers.com/movie/Last-Unicorn -The.

p. 14, "The animated version of *Cinderella*": Box Office History for Cinderella Movies," The Numbers, n.d., www.the-numbers.com/movie/Cinderella-(1950).

p. 14, "the live-action version of *Cinderella*": "Cinderella (2015)," The Numbers, n.d., www.the-numbers.com/movie/Cinderella-(2015).

p. 14, "Story was crucial to our evolution": Lisa Cron, *Wired for Story: The Writers Guide to Using Brain Science to Hook Readers from the Very First Sentence* (Berkeley, CA: Ten Speed Press, 2012), Introduction, iBooks.

p. 22, "The Romantics are very keen": Alain de Botton, "On Love (talk, Sydney Opera House, Australia, April 2016), www.sydneyoperahouse.com/digital/season/talks -and-ideas/alain-de-botton-on-love.html.

CHAPTER 2

p. 34, "There is nothing that strengthens the ego": Eckhart Tolle, *A New Earth: Awakening to Your Life's Purpose* (New York: Dutton, 2005), chap. 3, iBooks.

p. 34, "Scientific assessments reveal that the wishes": Bruce Lipton quoted in Craig Gustafson, "Bruce Lipton, Phd: The Jump from Cell Culture to Consciousness," *Integrative Medicine* 16, no. 6 (December 16, 2017): 44–50, www.ncbi.nlm.nih.gov /pmc/articles/PMC6438088/.

p. 35, "Of the downloaded behaviors acquired": Ibid.

p. 39, "The latest research supports the notion": Joe Dispenza, *Breaking the Habit of Being Yourself: How to Lose Your Mind and Create a New One* (Carlsbad, CA: Hay House, 2012), Introduction, iBooks.

p. 40, "If you are chasing joy and peace": T.S. Sathyanarayana Rao, M.R. Asha, K.S. Jagannatha Rao, and P. Vasudevaraju, "The Biochemistry of Belief," *Indian Journal of Psychiatry* 51, no. 4 (October–December 2009): 239–41, www.ncbi.nlm.nih.gov /pmc/articles/PMC2802367/.

CHAPTER 3

p. 49, "For the brain to rewire itself": Tara Swart, "The 4 Underlying Principles of Changing Your Brain," *Forbes*, May 27, 2018, www.forbes.com/sites/taraswart/2018/03/27 /the-4-underlying-principles-to-changing-your-brain/?sh=21cee1e65a71.

p. 51, "a belief is a thought that we've been attaching to": Byron Katie with Stephen Mitchell, *Loving What Is: Four Questions That Can Change Your Life* (New York: Three Rivers Press, 2003), chap. 1, Kindle.

p. 52, "a thought is harmless unless we believe it": Ibid, chap. 1, Kindle.

CHAPTER 4

p. 61, "95 percent of our thoughts": Jason Murdock, "Humans Have More Than 6,000 Thoughts per Day, Psychologists Discover," *Newsweek*, July 15, 2020, www.newsweek.com/humans-6000-thoughts-every-day-1517963.

p. 61, "The longer you focus upon something": Esther Hicks and Jerry Hicks, *The Law of Attraction: The Basics of the Teachings of Abraham* (Carlsbad, CA: Hay House, 2006), Part Two, Kindle.

p. 66, "The brain simply believes what you tell it most": Shad Helmstetter, *What to Say When You Talk to Your Self* (New York: Gallery Books, 2017), 9.

p. 66, "speaking to your mind": Marisa Peer, "Amazing Secrets of Your Mind (The Words You Use)," YouTube video, 8:33, October 11, 2019, www.youtube.com /watch?v=xSUfLyrhJME.

p. 73, "What we believe, we become": Bruce Lipton, "What Is Epigenetics?", 2021, www.brucelipton.com/what-epigenetics/.

p. 77, "The Universe responds to your vibrational offering": Esther Hicks and Jerry Hicks, *Ask and It Is Given: Learning to Manifest Your Desires* (Carlsbad, CA: Hay House, 2004), Process #4, Kindle.

CHAPTER 5

p. 82, "In the West, most of our physical needs": Alol Jha, "Where Belief is Born," *The Guardian*, June 30, 2005, www.theguardian.com/science/2005/jun/30/psychology .neuroscience.

p. 83, "I can promise you": Tory Eletto (nytherapist), "Choose Yourself," Instagram, May 18, 2021, www.instagram.com/p/CPA6A1vDUDu/.

p. 83, "not based on a condition": Lisa Kalmin, telephone interview with authors, June 25, 2021 (all quotations from Lisa Kalmin in this chapter are taken from this interview).

CHAPTER 6

p. 90, "To become masters of love": Miguel Ruiz with Janet Mills, *The Mastery of Love: A Practical Guide to the Art of Relationship* (San Rafael, California: Amber-Allen Publishing, 1999), chap. 1, iBooks.

p. 92, "unconscious image of familiar love": Harville Hendricks and Helen LaKelly Hunt, "What Is Imago?" Harville & Helen, 2021, harvilleandhelen.com/initiatives /what-is-imago/.

p. 95, "It changes how you decide to live": Brian Andreas, quoted by Tory Eletto (nytherapist), "It Changes How You Decide," Instagram, December 27, 2020, www.instagram.com/p/CJTP_F2DZwP/.

p. 96, "Authenticity is the daily practice": Brené Brown, *The Gifts of Imperfection: Let Go of Who You Think You're Supposed to Be and Embrace Who You Are* (Center City, MN: Hazelden Publishing, 2010), Guidepost #1, iBooks

CHAPTER 7

p. 99, "Expectation is the root of all heartache": Brad Sylvester, "Fact Check: Did Shakespeare Say 'Expectation Is the Root of All Heartache'?" Check Your Fact, September 25, 2019, checkyourfact.com/2019/09/25/fact-check-shakespeare -expectation-root-heartache/.

p. 102, "Expectations are more correlated to 'nice-to-haves'": Mark Groves, Zoom interview with authors, June 15, 2021 (all quotations from Mark Groves in this chapter are taken from this interview).

p. 110, "Expectations are narratives disguised as boundaries": Tory Eletto (nytherapist), "Expectations are narratives," Instagram, September 29, 2020, www.instagram.com /p/CFuALz9DNPD/.

CHAPTER 8

p. 117, "Little boys and little girls start off": Terrence Real, *I Don't Want to Talk About It: Overcoming the Secret Legacy of Male Depression* (New York: Scribner), chap. 5, iBooks.

p. 117, "gender stereotyping": University of Sussex, "Gender stereotyping may start as young as three months, study of babies' cries shows," ScienceDaily, www.sciencedaily .com/releases/2016/04/160422075235.htm (accessed September 19, 2021).

p. 117, "suicide rate for men in the United States": "Suicide," National Institute of Mental Health, n.d., www.nimh.nih.gov/health/statistics/suicide.

p. 118, "men are three times more likely": "Sex and Gender Differences in Substance Use," National Institute on Drug Abuse, April 13, 2021, www.drugabuse.gov /publications/research-reports/substance-use-in-women/sex-gender-differences-in -substance-use.

p. 118, "93 percent of prisoners": Alexia Cooper and Erica L. Smith, "Homicide Trends in the United States 1980–2008," U.S. Department of Justice, Bureau of Justice Statistics, November 2011, bjs.ojp.gov/content/pub/pdf/htus8008.pdf.

p. 119, "two times more likely": Dyfed Loesche, "The Prison Gender Gap," Statistica, October 23, 2017, www.statista.com/chart/11573/gender-of-inmates-in-us-federal -prisons-and-general-population/.

p. 121, "Unlike women, who are encouraged": Melanie Hamlett, "Men Have No Friends and Women Bear The Burden," *Harper's Bazaar*, May 2, 2019, www.harpersbazaar .com/culture/features/a27259689/toxic-masculinity-male-friendships -emotional-labor-men-rely-on-women/.

p. 122, "My wife and daughters": Quoted in Brené Brown, "Listening to Shame" (TED Talk, March 16, 2012), YouTube, 20:38, www.youtube.com/watch?v =psN1DORYYV0.

p. 124, "As hip and open-minded as they like to think they are": Ralph Gardner Jr., "Alpha Women, Beta Men," *New York Magazine*, November 7, 2003, nymag.com /nymetro/news/features/n_9495/.

CHAPTER 9

p. 128, "*Why Men Love Bitches*": Sherry Argov, *Why Men Love Bitches: From Doormat to Dreamgirl—A Woman's Guide to Holding Her Own in a Relationship* (New York: Adams Media, 2002).

p. 139, "Accept the fact that we don't have control": Pearl Flax, quoted in Kristine Felizar, "9 Types of Relationship Drama You're Too Old For," Bustle, January 11, 2017, www.bustle.com/p/9-types-of-drama-youre-too-old-to-be-dealing-with-in-a -relationship-27741.

CHAPTER 10

p. 146, "The question to ask yourself": Lisa Kalmin, telephone interview with authors, June 25, 2021 (all quotations from Lisa Kalmin in this chapter are taken from this interview).

p. 148, "smoke detector": Bessel van der Kolk, *The Body Keeps the Score: Brain, Mind, and Body in the Healing of Trauma* (New York: Penguin Books, 2014), Part 2, iBooks.

p. 148, "The active amygdala": Diane Musho Hamilton, "Calming Your Brain During Conflict," *Harvard Business Review*, December 22, 2015, hbr.org/2015/12 /calming-your-brain-during-conflict.

p. 149, "Popular Patterns": Esther Perel, "Fight Smarter: Avoid the Most Common Argument Patterns," n.d., www.estherperel.com/blog/fight-smarter-avoid-the -most-common-argument-patterns.

p. 151, "tactical empathy": Chris Voss with Tahl Raz, *Never Split the Difference: Negotiating as if Your Life Depended on It* (New York: HarperCollins, 2016), 52.

p. 158, "Apologizing for real": Lisa Kalmin, telephone interview with authors, June 25, 2021 (all quotations from Lisa Kalmin in this chapter are taken from this interview).

CHAPTER 11

p. 163, "racing and racing": Helen Rumbelow, "The Science Behind Broken Heart Syndrome," *The Times*, June 22, 2021, www.thetimes.co.uk/article/the-science -behind-broken-heart-syndrome-39dxswwj9.

p. 164, "The biological experience of breakups": Mark Groves, Zoom interview with authors, June 15, 2021 (all quotations from Mark Groves in this chapter are taken from this interview).

p. 168, "at greater risk of further cycling": Amber Vennum, Rachel Lindstrom, J. Kale Monk, and Rebekah Adams, "It's Complicated: The Continuity and Correlates of Cycling in Cohabiting and Marital Relationships," *Journal of Social and Personal Relationships* 31, no. 3 (2014): 410–20, retrieved from krex.ksu.edu.

p. 172, "Cleaning up our external environment": Rebecca Beaton, quoted in Kate Rope, "8 Secrets Why Women Love to Clean," *Real Simple*, August 29, 2014, www.realsimple.com/home-organizing/cleaning/love-clean.

p. 175, "clearing the weeds": Nada Vignjevic, telephone interview with authors, May 20, 2021 (all quotations from Nada Vignjevic in this chapter are taken from this interview).

p. 177, "As you build up your confidence": Victoria Gigante, "How to Rebuild After a Breakup," n.d., www.victoriagigante.com/how-to-rebuild-after-a-break-up/.

FURTHER READING

Basile, Giambattista. *The Cat Cinderella*, bookcandy.typepad.com/files/cinderella
-variants.pdf.

Beattie, Andrew. "Walt Disney: How Entertainment Became an Empire," Investopedia,
July 26, 2020, www.investopedia.com/articles/financial-theory/11/walt-disney
-entertainment-to-empire.asp.

Carlton, Genevieve. "In the Original Sleeping Beauty the King Is a Sexual Harasser
Who Forces Himself on the Princess," Ranker, August 22, 2019, www.ranker.com
/list/details-from-the-original-sleeping-beauty/genevieve-carlton.

Colier, Nancy. "Stop 'Shoulding' Yourself to Death, *Psychology Today*, April 6, 2013,
www.psychologytoday.com/us/blog/inviting-monkey-tea/201304/stop-shoulding
-yourself-death-0.

Denecke, Ludwig. "The Brothers Grimm," Britannica, last updated December 29, 2020,
www.britannica.com/biography/Brothers-Grimm.

Lipton, Bruce. *The Biology of Belief: Unleashing the Power of Consciousness, Matter &
Miracles* (Carlsbad, CA: Hay House, 2011).

Mary. "Cinderella: The Real Story," Book Review Page, February 7, 2016,
thebookreviewpage.wordpress.com/2016/02/07/cinderella-the-real-story/.

Mayo Clinic Staff. "Chronic Stress Puts Your Health at Risk," Mayo Clinic,
July 8, 2021, www.mayoclinic.org/healthy-lifestyle/stress-management/in-depth
/stress/art-20046037.

Perrault, Charles. *The Little Glass Slipper* (1697), www.pitt.edu/~dash/perrault06.html

Perrault, Charles. *Little Red Riding Hood* (1697), core.ecu.edu/engl/parillek
/littleredcinder.pdf.

Proctor, Bob. "The Secret to Living the Life You Want," Proctor Gallagher Institute, n.d.,
www.proctorgallagherinstitute.com/44551/the-secret-to-living-the-life-you-want.

Riley, Kathryn. "Romanticism: Historical Context of Romanticism," Fairy Tales: A Lamar Critical Edition, n.d., fairytalescriticaleditionlu.weebly.com/historical -context-of-romanticism.html.

Shamay-Tsoory, Simone G., Yasmin Tibi-Elhanany, and Judith Aharon-Peretz. "The Ventromedial Prefrontal Cortex Is Involved in Understanding Affective but Not Cognitive Theory of Mind Stories," *Social Neuroscience* 1, no. 3–4 (2006): 149–66, pubmed.ncbi.nlm.nih.gov/18633784/.

Sheek, Charles. "A Thousand Cinderellas," *Playbill*, June 10, 2005, www.playbill.com /article/a-thousand-cinderellas.

Speccoll, Robinson. "Grimms' Fairy Tales—December 2012," Newcastle University, Special Collections, December 27, 2012, blogs.ncl.ac.uk/speccoll/2012/12/27 /grimms-fairy-tales-december-2012/.

ACKNOWLEDGMENTS

I WOULD LIKE TO THANK, first and foremost, my writing partner and BFF Shannon. Writing this together has been so fun, so frustrating, so emotional, and so amazing. I couldn't have and would not have wanted to do it without you.

To my amazing family who have given me the foundation of my values and taught me about real love: I love all of you.

To my chosen family: Zaid, Andrew, Manu, Kevin, JB, Jared, Gregory, AK, Cervando, Mike, Jorge, Tanya, Esthero, D'Arcy, Maddy, Brad, John, Jennifer, Kio, Bobby, Mynxii, Nathan, Nicole, Sahara, and so many others. Thank you for your support, your love, and your belief in me.

To my transformational leaders Lynne and Lisa, without whom this book would not be possible.

And to all the people who participated in this book, especially Maggie and the entire team at Wonderwell. And a very special thank-you to our editor, Joanna. You're a fuckin' rock star. We did it! —*Beau*

Thank you, my sweet Beau, for your friendship, wisdom, love, laughs, late nights, early mornings, and everything in between while writing this book and beyond. My life is better because you are in it, and I am so grateful for everything we have—but most of all for the opportunity to share this book with you.

To our editor, Joanna Henry: thank you for your unwavering belief in us, your patience, and your deep understanding of our passion and voice. Maggie Langrick, you have had our backs every step of the way; thank you for pushing when we needed to be pushed and believing in our story. Thank you as well to the entire Wonderwell team: Jesmine Cham, Allison Serrell, and Morgan Krehbiel. (Sorry for all those cover revisions!)

For my mom, whose iron will, strength, and determination modeled me into the woman I am today. I am forever grateful. And for my dad, who stayed up many a late night after a long day to teach me how to be a better writer and communicator. Your patience and love showed me how to make my work stronger because you believed it could be—even when I didn't. My two little boys also deserve to be thanked. There were many nights when Mommy told you to go to bed so she could work, and you almost always did. But on the nights you didn't, you sat with me while I typed away, and those memories are some of the sweetest. And to Elizabeth and Glenn, you checked in on me and made me feel so loved through a very tough year.

Thank you to George. Our story is not the stuff of fairy tales, but it should be. I know your love, support, and gentle nature is forever.

To my girlfriends Theresa Sinclair, Tiffany Soper, Malania Dela Cruz, Rebecca Tay, Fiona Morrow, Tanya Clark, and Kim Peacock— you are the heroines of my life.

Thank you to Michael Green for deep relationship chats, Mark Groves for sharing your wisdom and time with us, and Steven Scarlett for cheering me on and giving me solid hugs when I needed them most. Brendan Bailey and Meriha Beaton, you shouldered the weight when I was struggling to keep up with it all; thank you for the heavy lifting.

And finally, thank you to the Universe, for revealing to me the beauty of selfless, endless love. —*Shannon*

ABOUT THE AUTHORS

Amanda Pratt

BEAU NELSON (he/him) is a creator. As an internationally recognized celebrity makeup artist, he has worked with women like Kristen Stewart, Zoë Kravitz, Christina Hendricks, and Iman. As a photographer/director, he has collaborated with legendary brands like Chanel, Dior, Violet Grey, and Chantecaille cosmetics. And as a multipassionate creative, he's been involved in countless other artistic endeavors from fragrance development to songwriting to visual art. Beau has spent years studying and practicing principles of personal transformation. He lives in Los Angeles, California.

SHANNON HETH (she/her) is a marketing and communications specialist who crafts creative strategy and stories for global brands. The president and founder of public relations agency Milk Creative Communications, her client work has appeared in *The New York Times*, *Vogue*, *FASHION*, and *The Washington Post*. An accomplished storyteller, Shannon has also penned a number of articles for newspapers and magazines, including a feature story in *The Globe and Mail* on her experience walking the runway at New York Fashion Week for the first time at the age of forty. She lives in Vancouver, British Columbia, with her two young sons.